CONTOURS

of

THE CITY

ATTYLA MOHYLNY

CONTOURS
of
THE CITY

CONTOURS OF THE CITY

by Attyla Mohylny

Translated from Ukrainian by Michael M. Naydan
With Translations of Five Poems by Virlana Tkacz and Wanda Phipps
Guest Introduction by Ivan Malkovych
Translator's introduction by Michael M. Naydan
Michael Naydan's Translations Edited by Larysa Bobrova

Book cover and interior layout by Max Mendor

© 2017, Michael M. Naydan

Cover Art © 2017, Max Mendor

© 2017, Glagoslav Publications B.V.

www.glagoslav.com

ISBN: 978-1-911414-57-5

A catalogue record for this book is available from the British Library.

This book is in copyright. No part of this publication may be reproduced, stored in a retrieval system or transmitted in any form or by any means without the prior permission in writing of the publisher, nor be otherwise circulated in any form of binding
or cover other than that in which it is published without a similar condition, including this condition, being imposed
on the subsequent purchaser.

ACKNOWLEDGMENTS

The following translations have previously been published: the cycle "Night Melodies" in AGNI 38, "Archipenko's Plasticity" (retitled here as "The Archipenko Sculpture") in the spring 1994 issue of Denver Quarterly. A partial manuscript of my translations of Mohylny's poetry was awarded the Eugene Kayden Meritorious Achievement Award in Translation from the University of Colorado in 1993. Extra special thanks to Larysa Bobrova for taking the time to go over my translations in meticulous detail and for improving them with her suggestions and corrections. I'm also grateful to Vasyl Byalyk for his excellent suggestions on the translation of the poem "My Blonde" as well as on my translation of Ivan Malkovych's guest introduction. Special thanks to Alla Perminova for her suggestions for emendations to the poem "An Evening in the Foothills."

Virlana Tkacz's and Wanda Phipps' translation of "Flying South through the Night" appeared in the literary journal Beacons: A Magazine of Literary Translations (1995) and the cycle "Beatles" appeared first in AGNI 36 (Fall 1992) and later in *A Hundred Years of Youth: A Bilingual Anthology of 20th Century Ukrainian Poetry*. Olha Luchuk and Michael M. Naydan, eds. Lviv: Litopys Press, 2000. All of the Tkacz/Phipps translations of Mohylny also appeared in *In a Different Light: A Bilingual Anthology of Ukrainian Literature Translated into English by Virlana Tkacz and Wanda Phipps as Performed by Yara Arts Group*. Olha Luchuk, ed. Lviv: Sribne Slovo, 2008.

Ivan Malkovych's essay "Dinastychnyi ukrains'kyi poet" (A Dynastic Ukrainian Poet) first appeared in Ukrainian in Attyla Mohylny, *Kyivski kontury*. Kyiv: AB-BA-BA-HA-LA-MA-HA, 2013. Part of Michael Naydan's introductory essay to this volume first appeared in Ukrainian in the journal Suchasnist in the July 1993 issue under the title "Dvoie ukrains'kykh poetiv: Oksana Zabuzhko i Attyla Mohyl'nyi" (Two Ukrainian Poets: Oksana Zabuzhko and Attyla Mohylny).

A NOTE ON THE TRANSLATORS

MICHAEL NAYDAN is the Woskob Family Professor of Ukrainian Studies at The Pennsylvania State University and translator, co-translator and/or editor of 40 books of translations from Ukrainian and Russian, more than 40 articles, and over 80 publications of translations in literary journals and anthologies.

VIRLANA TKACZ and WANDA PHIPPS have received the Agni Poetry Translation Prize, the National Theatre Translation Fund Award and 12 translation grants from the New York State Council on the Arts. Their translations have appeared in many literary journals and anthologies, and are integral to the theatre pieces created by Yara Arts Group.

WANDA PHIPPS is the author of the books *Field of Wanting: Poems of Desire* (BlazeVOX[books]) and *Wake-Up Calls: 66 Morning Poems* (Soft Skull Press). She received a New York Foundation for the Arts Poetry Fellowship. Her poems have appeared in over 100 literary magazines and numerous anthologies.

VIRLANA TKACZ heads the Yara Arts Group and has directed thirty original shows at La MaMa Theatre in New York, as well as in Kyiv, Lviv, Kharkiv, Bishkek, Ulaanbaatar and Ulan Ude. She received an NEA Poetry Translation Fellowship for her translations with Wanda of Serhiy Zhadan's poetry. www.brama.com/yara

LARYSA BOBROVA is a translation studies specialist, who served as Chair of the Translation Studies Department at the Horlivka Institute for Foreign Languages in Ukraine before coming to the US. She received her Ph.D. in Applied Linguistics from The Pennsylvania State University and is currently a Visiting Assistant Professor at the University of Miami, Oxford, OH where she teaches courses in ESL and in linguistics. Her main areas of research include cognitive semantics, conceptual metaphor, and second language acquisition.

CONTENTS

ACKNOWLEDGMENTS. 5

A NOTE ON THE TRANSLATORS 6

A DYNASTIC KYIVAN POET BY IVAN MALKOVYCH 9

CONTOURS OF CONSCIOUSNESS:
THE POETRY OF ATTYLA MOHYLNY 15

CONTOURS OF THE CITY 21

    A SHIELD MADE OF STEEL 23

        BLACK LAKES. 23

        A SCORCHING NOON 26

        RANDOM MOVEMENT. 28

        THE BEATLES 29

        FLEETING RECOLLECTIONS 33

        NIGHT MELODIES 36

        A STORMY SEASON 41

        THE CATHEDRAL. 45

    BENEATH THE BRIGHT SUN 50

        SONG TO THE SUN 50

        ARIAS 51

        FAR AWAY 53

        AN ADVENTURE 56

        THE SHIPSAILING SONG 58

        THE MIDDLE AGES 66

        A CARAVAN. 70

    EVENINGS. TWILIGHT. IMPRESSIONS. 74

        PRELUDE 74

        JOURNEYS 75

        A GOLD-BEARING SONNET 76

- IN THE SOUTH 77
- A MAGIC ACT 78
- THE LAST APPRENTICE OF MAGISTER KNECHT 79
- BATTLE 80
- THE MIRAGE 81
- IMPROVISATION 82
- SPANISH MELODIES 83
- JOAN OF ARC 84
- THE SEASONS ON ST. ANDREW'S DESCENT 85
- THE WINTER OF OUR CITY 88
- THE END OF A GLOOMY DAY 91
- CIRCULATION 92
- SAVE OUR SOUL 93
- A REALLY BRIGHT DAWN 94
- IN A GALLOP BENEATH THE MOON 95
- DIAPHANOUS MORNING 96
- A RENAISSANCE 97
- COFFEE HOUSES 101
- THE ARCHIPENKO SCULPTURE 104
- REVERIES 105
- MINIATURE SKETCHES 109

OTHER POEMS 116
- MY BLONDE 116
- AN EVENING IN THE FOOTHILLS 119

TRANSLATIONS BY VIRLANA TKACZ
AND WANDA PHIPPS 121
- BLOND 121
- A BRIDGE CROSSES THE POND 125
- FLYING SOUTH THROUGH THE NIGHT 126
- BEATLES 127
- SPONTANEOUS MOTION 131

A DYNASTIC KYIVAN POET

Attyla Mohylny happened to transverse his creative path in a cloak of invisibility common for a Ukrainian artist. There are very few articles about his books and very little mention of him in the press. Fortunately, over the past two or three years in conversations with several Americans interested in Ukrainian poetry Attyla's name suddenly and consistently has been uttered in ecstatic reveries about English translations of his poems that were marvelously congruent with a Western sensibility. This is not surprising because Attyla is a poet of Ukraine's largest megalopolis, and in his poetry there are numerous images and feelings that in one way or another are compatible with those of American beatniks. Toward the end of his life Attyla even acquired the real appearance of a beatnik, but not as a result of some kind of scandalous behavior, but rather just because something had gone wrong in his life.

However, in his poetry—with bright platoons of horseback riders, with solemn princely military drills, and the Polovtsian eyes of waitresses in Kyiv's cafes—I primarily feel an involuntary echo of the poets Yuri Darahan and Olexander Olzhych. And, of course, the early poetry of Bohdan Ihor Antonych, but somehow a very Kyivan Antonych. In Attyla's last poetry there is poignant Mandelstamian despair... Kyiv in Attyla's poetry becomes a full-blooded Ukraine-centered Mecca. The language of his poems is precise, noble, decisive, impetuous. Ukrainian princes would have spoken this way when, once setting off for dangerous military or hunting exercises, they might unexpectedly have appeared in modern-day Kyiv.

Attyla Mohylny was born September 16, 1963 in Kyiv and died September 3, 2008 in the city he loved and called home his entire abbreviated life. He was one of the most talented of the "Eighties" generation of writers and one of the very few dynastic poets of Kyiv. His father—the poet Viktor Mohylny—is better known to the wider community as the great children's poet Vit Vitko.

Attyla graduated from the philological faculty of Taras Shevchenko Kyiv State University. For some time he taught there and taught as well in the Ukrainian studies program at the University of Warsaw. He studied Persian language and culture at the University of Tadjikistan, worked in television, in the Mohyla Academy Collegium, and as an editor for the newspaper Voice of Ukraine.

He is the author of two collections of poetry: *Tumbler Pigeons over the Rooftops* (1987) and *The Outlines of the City* (1991). He is also the author of the original children's book *Mavka and the Ant Prince* (1988, 2006).

We were classmates and close friends in school. For two years we even shared an apartment together. Attyla was a native of Kyiv, but his Hungarian mother's blood probably added to his character a special "tzimmes" that demanded absolute freedom.

We met each other first at our entrance exams to the university. Attyla distinguished me from among the other applicants by my "Angela Davis" hair and a scar on my hand. With his zealous poetic imagination he somehow treated me like a young Don Juan gypsy poet. This, in fact, clearly was characteristic of his worldview. Attylka (as we called him by the diminutive form of his name) loved creating romantic myths.

We often read the same books, and in our shared apartment listened to the same music—from the Beatles to classical symphonies. A third classmate, the poet Ihor Malenky, joined us there. It was as if we formed a kind of trio—three "M's." We managed to save a copy of our jointly penned "triad" poem, written under the pseudonym of Ivan Troyan. We wrote it during student military prep classes and called it "Guidelines for Cleaning Weapons and Shoes":

> Don't clean your shoes like a rifle for shooting
> because right when you move beyond all the rivers
> in the early morning— drums lie there
> with drumsticks stuck into the ground
> they'll quietly count all who have fallen
> monotonically like dust on sandals...

In 1983 we were on summer student training at a young pioneer camp at the seaside near Gelendzhik not far from Novorossisk, where the vast majority of children—descendants of Kuban Cossacks—spoke to each other mainly in Ukrainian. On this comforting occasion Attylka and I (it was actually his idea) introduced Ukrainian commands in our detachments. "Platoon! Straighten up! Attention!" Along with a few other commands. This sounded especially stirring coming from the lips of a boy from Moscow, whom we specifically chose as head of the unit. But then someone snitched on us and our "military Ukrainization" on the territory occupied by our "brother Slavs" was harshly abbreviated....

We, of course, read our just written poems to each other. We praised or criticized each other's work, seasoning everything with a dose of constant irony. To his last days Attyla liked to jot down poems on cigarette packs and matchbooks. Attyla's character was reserved and quite secretive rather than open. Once he brought home some hand-rolled cigarettes filled with marijuana, but it, fortunately, had no effect on me. Attylka toyed with this new hobby just for a day or two—poetry became "ingrained" inside him a hundred times stronger.

In addition to poetry, Attylka was crazy over the opposite sex. He could fall in love at half a glance (but usually not for very long). Without an inkling of remorse he could go after some other guy's girlfriend. He once visited me in Bereziv, where later in our house (this was during the dark times of the USSR), we secretly baptized his young poet wife (I was the "godmother's" godfather). And before that his only children's tale was "baptized"—while working in the Veselka children's publishing house I urged Attylka to write a children's book (that's when his "Mavka and the Ant Prince" was published in an edition of nearly two hundred thousand copies). Much later, two years before he passed away, I managed to reissue a revised version of "Mavka..." in my A-BA-BA-HA-LA-MA-HA Publishing House. Over the last ten to twelve years of his earthly journey Attyla dropped by several times a week at my A-BA-BA-HA-LA-MA-HA office in downtown Kyiv for a coffee and a smoke....

I've long loved his poems and know several by heart. I've even read them in the Union of Writers author's evenings at the end of the late nineties at the extremely rare during his lifetime. I sincerely consider this restless (and currently still quite underappreciated) Kyiv wanderer one of the most interesting and most identifiable Ukrainian poets of the end of the second millennium. I have a secret hope that, like the poets Bohdan Ihor Antonych or Mykhail Semenko, interest in Attyla's poetry will be sparked among a young readership.

For a better understanding of the environment in which Attyla grew, I'll give a brief sketch of his father—Viktor Mohylny, a talented poet in his own right and a prominent Ukrainian philatelist. The author of the essay is Vasyl Ovsiyenko:

"In the early 1960s, after decades of anti-Ukrainian pogroms, informed Ukrainians in Kyiv felt humiliated, estranged. Probably there were very few informed Ukrainian families—on those islands of independence. One of them was the Mohylny family—Viktor and his wife Aurelia (who was Hungarian and from the Western Ukrainian city of Uzhhorod and who became a Ukrainian patriot).

A mighty Ukrainian spirit dominated in the Mohylny home in Chokolivka. The walls were covered everywhere with Ukrainian words and autographs, with Ukrainian books and cultural artifacts lying everywhere. An informal literary circle was active there, where Ukrainian might surged. It consisted of a cohort that created a critical mass of Ukrainianness. It appeared in the sixties, and later—in the human rights movement and in the struggle for independence at the cusp of the 1980s-1990s. In these kinds of families children grew up for whom it was extremely difficult to remain Ukrainians in a totally Russified and amorally aggressive environment. This is how Viktor's son, the poet Attyla Mohylny, Viktor's daughter Dzvinka, and his grandchildren Bohdan and Yaropolk grew.

Viktor Mohylny was unable to acquire a higher education because at the university entrance exams, being a truthful individual, he interpreted Shevchenko's Kateryna (from his long poem "Kateryna") as an image of Ukraine, violated by a Russian soldier.

Viktor, as a proscribed writer, was not permitted to publish a single poetry book. Only in the 1980s when his grandson was born did his children's books come out under the pseudonym of Vit Vitko: "The Snail-Tiny Ant," "Swing Once, Swing Twice" and in 1999 a samizdat collection "Csokolivka, csokolj meg! or The Bitten Apple" under the bizarre pseudonym of Vykhtir Orkhlyn (in Hungarian: Chokolivka, Kiss Me!). His poetic language is refined, his metaphors expressive and paradoxical. His poetry is outwardly non-political, but does manage to express a Ukrainian mentality.

And this worker of "Leninska Kuznya" (Lenin's Forge), where he worked for 25 years, became proscribed because of the fact that he participated in the "Brama" (The Gate) literary workshop of workers' poets in the Club of Creative Youth. On May 22, 1967 Viktor Mohylny was among four arrested by KGB agents near the Taras Shevchenko monument in Kyiv. At that time Mykola Plakhotniuk summoned others to go there together to free them. Close to midnight about 600 followers of Shevchenko went to the Central Committee of the Communist Party and managed to negotiate the release of the detainees. It was there for the first time Ukrainians chanted "hanba" (shame) in unison. This word later became a verbal pickaxe to gouge at the colonial regime. There was a lone tourist there—a German—who ran up to them and asked: "Was ist hanba?"

You had to be not of the easily frightened dozen to go to the former Simon Petlura supporter and political prisoner with twenty years of "experience" Borys Antonenko-Davydovych. Viktor did that together with Oles Shevchenko (a well-known dissident and Attyla's godfather) and Hryts Tymenko. Hryts went missing without a trace when he began to prepare the book by Ukrainian dissident Ivan Dziuba *Internationalism or Russification?* In 1968 an article by Antonenko-Davydovych appeared in the newspaper Literary Ukraine entitled "A Letter that is Mourned" (about the banned by the Soviets Ukrainian letter "г" (g) in which the author cited an earlier article by Viktor Mohylny in Literary Ukraine dated October 1, 1965 under the title "The Trouble with Consonants"). Deputy editor Marharita Malinovska intentionally published the rebellious article and announced a discussion of the feasibility of a return to the Ukrainian alphabet of the banned letter.

In the next issue Doctor of Philology Vitaly Rusanovsky, whom for the latter's support of the Russification "theory of bilingualism," Ivan Bilodid nicknamed "Russofather," made a pronouncement: "There's Nothing to be Sad About." The debate was stopped in its tracks.

Vsevolod Hantsov, a well-known linguist in the 1920s and the only surviving member of the "SVU" (League for the Liberation of Ukraine) court case,1 lived in Chernihiv. Mohylny sent him a letter asking for explanations of certain philological issues. This was at a time when everyone avoided Hantsov in fear. The scholar answered him with a substantive letter—and that for him proved to be strong moral support.

Once again Viktor Mohylny was "lustrated" in the case of Oles Shevchenko, Vitaly Shevchenko, and Stepan Khmara. During a search on March 31, 1980 of Oles's home they discovered a poem "Biography (I am frightened...)." There were accusations that the author was spreading a "defamatory, anti-Soviet document." At that time Oles told the investigator that he had stolen the poem: the owner was not home, and his wife was doing the wash. He liked the poem lying on the table and put it in his pocket. Vladimir Shevchenko observed at an evening gathering that Mohylny at their trial in Lviv aggressively demanded a clarification to him

---

1   In 1930 at a show trial in Kharkiv Hantsov received a prison term of eight years during Stalin's crackdown against Ukrainian intellectuals.

of which lines of the poem and what exactly are "defamatory" about them. The judge spoke in Russian to him, and Mohylny acting as if he didn't understand asked him in Ukrainian: "Pardon me?" And he did so several times. In this way he forced the judge to speak Ukrainian to him.

The same day, during a search of Mohylny's home, 34 documents were seized—works of samizdat, "The Declaration" and "Memorandum Number 1" of the Ukrainian Helsinki Group, books, notebooks, manuscripts, letters, and a typewriter. On February 21, 1981, according to the Director of the State Archive of the Security Service Alexander Pshennykov, "for nationalistic statements and for writing poetry with an ideologically harmful content V.M. Mohylny was put under preventive care by the Fifth Department of the KGB of the Ukrainian SSR as a result of a conversation on the premises of the KGB with the verdict of an official warning"....

It is worth knowing that independence did not fall from heaven to Ukrainians. It depended on specific people who endured intense pressure from the occupiers and during the harshest times of ruin were living bearers of the Ukrainian spirit."

—Ivan Malkovych
—Translated by Michael M. Naydan

CONTOURS OF CONSCIOUSNESS: THE POETRY OF ATTYLA MOHYLNY

Attyla Mohylny, son of the Ukrainian poet Vit Vitko, was born on September 16, 1963 in Kyiv, Ukraine, and died all too prematurely on September 3, 2008 at the age of 45. Mohylny, whose last name comes from the Ukrainian word "mohyla"—meaning "grave" or "mound," sadly became the realized metaphor of his personal onomastic origins.

He completed his philology degree at Kyiv State University and then continued his studies while working in Dushanbe, Tadzhikistan, first as a group leader of The Young Pioneers, then as a teacher in the Medical Institute until 1985. Following his travels to Tadzhikistan, in Kyiv he tried his hand at journalism for the newspaper Evening Kyiv. Since then Mohylny had an off and on career as a teacher and journalist. He worked as an editor in the Molod Publishing House, and from 1987 taught occasionally at Kyiv and Warsaw Universities. He worked in television, writing film scripts for children's shows. He authored two books of poetry early in his career: *Tumbler Pigeons above the Rooftops* (1987) and *Contours of the City* (1991) as well as the text for the exquisite children's book *Mavka and the Ant King* in 2006. He continued to work on writing short stories and a novel before his death.

The poet told me that he was named after a saint Attyla and not the Hun of more historical renown. Mohyla was a poet of the city, one of the late 1980s generation of urban intellectuals who lived and breathed the pulsating rhythms of the capital city of Kyiv's urban landscapes. While he found inspiration in the cityscapes, he did so in unique ways with a poetic voice distinctly different from traditional Ukrainian rhymed and metered poetry. He transformed elements of the city into scenes that turned the seemingly mundane into the mystical. Mohylny's essential quest was one of self-definition. His lyrical "I" is akin to a camera roving over the cityscape and through the coffee shops, where his generation formulated its outlook on life in heated daily discussions in the shadows of Brezhnev's hypocritical and hollow policy of the "friendship of nations." For these young Ukrainians the coffee houses during their young adulthood, and not the officially sanctioned and heavily censored journals, provided the locus for intellectual life. It was in these coffee shops where they discovered life, love, and the roots of their individuality as well as their own inner spirit. It is no surprise, too, that he titles one of his cycles "Beatles," precisely because their music represented one of the strongest emblems of freedom for generations of East Europeans.

The liner notes to Mohylny's second book *Contours of the City* (*Obrysy mista*; 1991), which also could be translated as *Outlines*, succinctly articulate the poet's quest: "This is not a monologue, but a dialogue with his (the poet's) contemporaries, the searching for what unifies people into a single generation, for what we call universal human values." Mohylny's search is not among the petrified icons of Ukrainian history such as the Kozak leaders Bohdan Khmelnytsky and Ivan Mazepa, who fought for Ukrainian independence from the Russians and Poles. Instead, he seeks the past in a transcendent, mythical sense. For example, in the cycle "Arias," the poet celebrates a scene of weary men returning from the steppe to their women with their "hot white legs" and "warm pink breasts," who wait to wrap their bodies around their returning warriors. While the eroticism is overt in this poem, the poem is really more about living as an individual, about the self-definition of a man via the ancestral shadows of his distant historical past, about his humanness, about his empowerment of the self.

Mohylny presents a lyric persona in his collection unusual for the Ukrainian and Slavic poetic tradition. He writes in a loose free verse style that projects a roaming consciousness, with a tenacity, with a childlike quality, with the spiritual longing of someone cut loose from an umbilical cord with an unquenchable thirst for experience. That consciousness is elusive, fleeting, constantly shifting. We are given to perceive the emotionality of his lyrical "I" in a fragmented, piecemeal way. The poems rapidly oscillate with extraordinary verbal tactility, much in the same way that Impressionist paintings can vibrate to allow us to see what the artist envisions through his unique perspective. In the poetry we are left with an emotional imprint of these moments of flowing consciousness captured in time.

Mohylny poses the questions that poets and philosophers have always posed: life, love, consciousness, being, eternity. He seeks the answers in the world around him, in the shadows, the lights and contours of the city that vibrate with the imprint of the past, shimmering simultaneously in his lyrical present. To borrow some of his own metaphors, memory provides a bridge, a slipstream to the past to help him define himself in his interpreted world. The ineluctability of music has that ability to capture the essence of the sorrow of his lonely quest, which is temporarily overcome by bright moments of interconnectedness with others. These motifs of brooding neo-Romantic loneliness and journey abound in his poems. He constantly takes to the streets, to the trams, to ships, to planes. He wanders to the coffee houses, along familiar paths, seeking something, constantly pondering, writing verse. Spring always turns to autumn leaves in the seemingly unending cycle of love and loss. Yet the poet continually finds strength in the world around him despite its often doleful nature. The cycle "Black Lakes" provides an appropriate microcosmic glimpse into Mohylny's created poetic world. Throughout the poem the "I" and "you" attempt to interact, to become a "we." Sometimes the "you" is his love, other times a projected image of the self. But the poet's "I" has no control over where this creative process will lead him. The trail of dreams takes him to the past, where cutters arrive amid yellowed leaves and depart off into the distance. They provide a constant flow of people, experiences and memories into and out of his life. This is a past where his love still lives in the recollections of his youth. The poet compares people to migrating birds that descend onto the damp, dark "lake" of the city. The stopover is transitory, the very nature of life on earth, barely long enough to rest until warmer climes can be reached. In the same way as the birds, people seek temporary respite and warmth in each other's company. In a coda closure, the black reflections after the rain on the "lakes" strewn with autumn leaves are all that remains at the end of the poem.

    A cycle such as "Night Melodies" offers a similar roving consciousness with the typical "I" interacting with the memory and reality of a "you." It begins with music and a reference that anchors the poem in time:

> Do you hear the guys from Liverpool singing?
> You don't understand the words,
> but you know the feelings.
> And now you walk along the street
> your love beside you.

Mohylny intersperses philosophical musings throughout the cycle. In the second part, the poet shifts from musings in a coffee shop on his loneliness, to his bittersweet lost youth, to a parching thirst in the middle of the night, to the radio where he seeks comfort with the music of Amadeus and reconciliation for his fate in the art of Ludwig. The telephone, another kind of technological wonder that transmits the music of the human voice, and which should offer a means to link with another individual, provides nothing but a banal snatch of conversation with the Beatle John Lennon: "John, is it snowing where you are, too?" In the third part of the cycle the poet attempts to transcend his self into his projected other and to achieve a sense of interconnectedness with his countrymen. In the poet's words: "The voice of a nation is the voice of God." That collective Ukrainian voice appears to the poet via memory in part four, where those wounded in battle, where gallows, where bloodied swords awaited the poet, who has passed them all by, by virtue of his youth and time of birth too late in the century.

In the final segment, the poet mentally transports himself into the role of a parachutist leaping from his plane onto the city with tracer bullets shooting up at him into the night sky. He comes to his senses from this dream state in a room with his love sleeping bundled in a blanket. He awakens before the parachute hits, so the dreamer in his dream state is jolted back into his reality.

While Mohylny offers bits of Kyivan realia in his poems, and makes links to his collective and individual "Ukrainianness" and past, he articulates a vision of his immediate present vibrant with life. He tests his life with all its uncertainty. His persona calls out: this is me, this is who I am at this point in time. And the journey to self-realization begins, repeats with variations, and continues, for this is the very nature of life.

The poetry of Mohylny in this exquisite collection, which was largely overlooked when it first appeared, certainly deserves a wider audience both in Mohylny's homeland where he is all but forgotten as well as in the wider world. While it, unfortunately, might be described as a one-hit wonder because of the poet's premature death, it remains a brilliant hit for all time.

A PERSONAL NOTE ON THE POET

I first met Attyla during an extended stay in Kyiv in 1993 with the Ukrainian writer Oksana Zabuzhko, whom I had met a few years previous to that at a Ukrainian studies conference at the University of Illinois. Oksana introduced me to him. Attyla, who was immediately quite friendly, suggested along with Oksana that the three of us take an overnight trip to the union of writer's retreat in Irpin just outside of Kyiv to experience the Ukrainian countryside. You get there to the sylvan outpost of literary culture nestled next to a tiny village by slow, dingy commuter train. This was a popular stop for many writers during Soviet times. Boris Pasternak and so many other great writers frequented it in earlier times to commune with pristine nature. Attyla immediately struck me as a childlike, mildly idiosyncratic fellow. He was slight of build with narrow shoulders, with a dark downward drooping mustache that seemed too big and out of place on his boyish face. He looked much younger than his age at that time. The mustache seemed to be a strategy to make himself look older. I vividly recall a quirky incident as we were waiting on a platform for the *elektrychka*, the electric local commuter train, to Irpin. Somehow Attyla's shoe accidentally tapped the shoe of a teenage girl, who was walking past us. The girl continued to walk away without paying much attention to the minor incident. Attyla had a different reaction. He immediately chased after her, imploring that she tap his shoe with hers, otherwise, he said, they would get into an argument. Attyla's superstitious belief came to be realized all too soon. He insisted so persistently, albeit politely, that she eventually raised her voice to him to leave her alone and moved as far away from him on the platform as she possibly could, shouting out that she was not going to tap his shoe. It was just one of those humorous moments, of course, that you always remember with a smile. I also recall one other interesting occasion during my visit with Attyla. Late in the evening he decided we should start a small bonfire in the woods on the grounds of the writer's retreat. He seemed quite adept at making bonfires, so Oksana and I sat back and watched him as he chain-smoked and gathered twigs, brambles and branches into a pile. We politely refused swigs of *horilka* (Ukrainian vodka) from a bottle he had brought with him, but he continued to take portions from it for himself. He seemed to be on the tipsy side though in control of his faculties. At one point during the building of the bonfire he threw a log onto it that somehow shot up smoke, ash and sparks at Oksana. Oksana jumped back, shouted out something like *oi, blin, chort* (oh crap, damn) brushed the ashes off her dress and implored him to stop and not ruin her dress. She calmed down quickly, and he managed to sober up immediately and not shoot any more sparks at her from the fire. It was a chilly evening, so we ended up appreciating the fire's warmth.

CONTOURS OF THE CITY

*Neighborhoods
that I perhaps will never forget.
And these courtyards
that remember our strumming guitars
with us walking from here
alone,
relying just on happiness
and the paltry truth
of our streets.*

*And time to time
each of us returned,
so that we could
press our shoulders
so strongly
to the firm walls
of these five-story buildings.*

*And perhaps
the greatest truthfulness
of the outer edges of Kyiv
is that
no one ever asked
where we were going.*

A SHIELD MADE OF STEEL

BLACK LAKES

A Cycle

    1.
I am not conscious of what I'm doing:[2]
a string of dreams
drawn between the past and me,
but I'm returning to the past
where cutters first
enter the waters of a bay
beneath yellow leaves —
lead and steel, and from above —
the sluggish cutters
and the stirring of waters in the slipstream.

I love you, my love.
Fog settles
in heavy droplets on the metal.

Go with me,
so that I do not return.
Autumn —
this is the flare of the forest edge in the fog
and the fast-moving silhouettes of the cutters
turned in the distance.

    2.
Melody and sorrow remain.
Look,
this is you and me,
this is the day
we love one another,

---

2   This line can also be read literally as: "I'm not conscious of what I create."

this is a world
where the voices of our youth
stretched steel rigging
over the bay,
over the cutters with paint scratched off,
over trains that brought the first ones.

Disembark onto this bridge
and we will call it memory.

When the last ones go,
only sorrow will remain,
like wine steeped in grass:
a window —this is the inevitability of glass
in front of which we stop.

    3.
The city at night
is a lake for migrating birds.
They descend into its lights,
and the water of shadows
closes above them.

Turning over at midnight we see:
a gray gloom strewn over the city
like the dust of embers on a bonfire.
We blaze through them.

Lead me along this path:
the blades of swords
leave their nests
(the time for flying south —the time for partings):
an all too gruff host,
but I must be there.

The movement in rows
as though a beast turned over:
the blackness of steel

creates reflections on the lake.
In the depth of the waters —
a transparent flow
and an autumnal bay
strewn with multicolored leaves.

A SCORCHING NOON

A Cycle

   1.
Towns — stations.

Rails covered with dust,
open space,
where there is the scent of herbs and the sleepy voice
of diesel engines.

(Sleep is the longest state
of our stay on earth,
and the railroads save us).
The model for our national character —
young provincial lions,
but there aren't enough diesel engines for all of them.

Our Nevada and our California.
Our fair-haired film stars
in station snack counters
waiting for packed trains.

   2.
The land of our sorrow.

This year's cobweb is above the platform
and the outlines of a naked body
through sheer calico drapes.

The long night will return the trains.

With a tigress's gait along the lonely platform:
young thighs tear bikini briefs —
thirst:

the white foam of Cyprus[3]
in tight bikini briefs.
...A spring of hopes,
a spring of great expectations...

        3.

The heavy velvet of rain
covers this land,
it is in the rain
we have to return:
only oblivion is inexhaustible.

We will return as apples from our own garden:
the velvet season continues,
the season of lights in broken train cars.

Women at the crossings —
are like the gaping mouths of night,
yelling to us.

---

[3] An epithet for Aphrodite, whose favorite abode was on the island of Cyprus.

RANDOM MOVEMENT

Slush in the outer edges of the city.

You stand in an empty park
with a pine branch in your hands.

We descend the steps to the pond:
to a dock with rowboats —
in the shadow of willows, that's why
we can't see the moon from here,
just colored sparkles
and the blue branch of a pine
swaying on the waves.

... Your lips, wet from the evening rain,
seek me...

... Tips of lit cigarettes
flash past on the dock...

... In the slushy outer edges of the city
I find your love...

We go inside ourselves
the way we wade into water.
Our fingers intertwined carelessly,
and with your free hand
you lift your skirt higher and higher
clenching it into your hand.
Through pine needles, chips and leaves
that sway on the surface,
we go deeper and deeper,
raking away the debris with our hands
that the waves carry to us.

THE BEATLES

          I.
I want to tell you all about
how we used to be in love,
queen of my life at sixteen.

We used to see each other
in the alleys of groves,
then there was school,
and factories after the work shift,
and pretty teenage princesses
ready to love the whole world,
that's why
our neighborhood
overflowed in sunlight
with hot blood meandering
in its veins.

And we made love
in the grove next-door,
where, while lying in the tall grass around the stadium,
we listened to the neighborhood of those princesses
fall asleep,
and we watched the lights go out of buildings
in the distance.

And when it seemed to us
that we were barely residents here,
we fell in love,
and back then our desire to change
                   the world was great,
and back then our town seemed great,
and our love too.

2.
When this music of the Liverpoolers plays
with my palm resting on your breast,
I see passion awakening
            in your eyes,
and I understand
that this music is telling us that
the city is coming alive in the morning
as we set off to work,
with droplets of dew flying off the chestnuts,
and saying farewell
wrapped in my arms
you talk to me about love,
though, for certain,
we'll never see each other again.

My city gave you to me,
and in the morning you disappear in its bustle,
and right at the moment of parting
your tangled hair flashes in the wind
and your clothes
wind around your body
that belongs not to me anymore,
but to the burning and thirsting music of the Liverpoolers.

3.
I don't have enough words
when I want to write about you.

I remember our childhood,
when, between flashes of the sun —
people, busy with their own affairs,
blossoming trees
and trucks
that on their tires have collected
not just the reddish dust of the town's outer edges,
but all the legends of the road,
straight and bare,

that have been lost somewhere beyond the horizon.

If someday
we put our lives to music,
it will be the music of dust, brick and road oil,
where the greatest poetry
was us.

        4.
Take it from me,
Beatles —
this is our sweet-smelling
youth, like an open window
in the empty room of mass art
and sterilized
classical music
but you hear —
the neighborhood is alive,
people, cats and trees alive,
the great sun alive above our neighborhood,
songs are alive, and that is why
you are taking your clothes off —
your jeans and sweater fly off into the corner
and without your clothes
you look so womanly
that I begin to love
your easy, timid movements
and the reserved joy of premonition
that clouded your eyes.
Take it from me,
Beatles —
this is our youth,
though we'll write about our love
ourselves.

        5.
... I see the boys from our neighborhood
and I think: we'll outshine those Liverpoolers —

our guitars play our own music
and our lips utter our own words
and, perhaps, it's not particularly that beautiful yet,
but these songs are about us —
how we love,
how we learn to make adjustments in fights,
breaking blows,
and how, slowly, mature to the words
Struggle and Homeland,
and how the hearts of our lovers beat,
overlapping the music of the Liverpoolers,
and I think
that our own music is present in our neighborhoods
and we grope for it.

FLEETING RECOLLECTIONS

1.

Ukraine began with Vidradny,[4]
surrounded by vacant land,
where in the shells of broken cars
brambles and legends grew,

where in the morning
fireflies in black arrows
flew out of dovecotes,
where the roofs smoked from the heat
and shadows moved along the roofs,
playing guitars and harmonicas.

From Vidradny,
where we were cast
from various ends of the world—
Spain, Solomyanka and Kurenivka,
Duklya and Mysholovka,
Rostov and Chokolivka,
and from which the shout of trains
tore us
at Chata-Volynska.

2.

Somewhere long ago
in the knocking of wheels
and in the green foam of soft speech at the train stations,
or in the twisted alleys of Druhy Sad,
or in the middle of the bridge to Trukhaniv
I met this girl,

---

4   An industrial district of Kyiv where Mohylny's parents live and where he grew up. The name translates as "joyful." The district originally was open farmland. The industrial buildings were built in Soviet times in the 1950s and 1960s along with dull-looking low-rise housing complexes.

because I remember
the cold touch of her hands
and the unexpected openness of her lips and eyes.

The name changed,
the face changed,
but all the same
the white sand makes her golden,
and her lips utter
words from the Book of Life.

3.

I don't know
what keeps me here—
the heavy buildings
that at night like tankers
float out from the boundless sky,
the light of streetlamps,
intertwined through golden paths
into the branches of trees,
or those, who with rough faces,
like lizards, scurry under the southern sun
politely humming about things to do
and shortly take the folks
to Odessa who had just dropped by,
so there would be no little misunderstanding
beneath the burning sun of Vidradny.

4.

The white walls of the factories
have become overgrown with ivy and vines,
the balconies and window frames have been colored
in red, green and blue,
and now you can
tear off a branch of tart St. John's Wort
among the small pine trees near the car-repair shop
and, rubbing it in your fingers,
recall

the night, far from this alley,
when cigarettes burn lips
and a barely familiar woman
in a black evening dress
sings about
how our youth forever goes
at a light pace,
an amulet gleaming on her neck.

       5.
The rabble, that rendered this land habitable,
was assembled by people
who came individually or in groups
and brought with them
the seeds of wild plants,
tenacious eyes of various colors
and wondrous words and names,
permeated with liquor, horses and the sea.
And here,
where in all four directions
Ukraine began,
they slapped shivs, switch blades, machetes,
    and shanks into tables
and went to spin around their three work shifts,
with pigeons and cherry trees populating
all of no one's lands of the neighborhood.

NIGHT MELODIES

A Cycle

I.

Do you hear the guys from Liverpool singing?
You don't understand the words,
but you know the feelings.
And now you walk along the street
your love beside you.
Stop and think,
in the end
it doesn't mean anything
to think about it anyway.
Yesterday everything was truth.
Today —it's history.
Turn on the music —
This is the gold of those who have none,
This is the Homeland of those on the road,
This is the nation of those who thirsted for battle, —
Turn on the music.
And ponder
why we love history so:
in the boundlessness of time
your tiny part is not worth the game,
but you will begin it.
Your love is beautiful,
the street along which you walk
is lined with trees,
and looking back, you see
children running to school,
and the painted edges of sidewalks and picket fences
painted white.
You understand: it's spring.
The perspiration of love floods your eyes
as ecstasy passes.
Take this moment with you
and start along the road.

From this day on
you are two,
yet time shows no mercy.

   2.
You leave work
and in a store on the corner,
leaning your elbows on a table,
drink a cup of coffee.
Friend, look:
why are you so lonely?
Your youth has passed,
no one needs your maturity,
your future is cloudless.
At night you wake up
and feel thirsty:
the sensation
that you've been executed by firing squad.
You get up and go to the kitchen,
gulp something
and turn on the radio:
"Amadeus, give me comfort."
"Ludwig, reconcile me with fate."
"John, is it snowing where you are, too?"
Friend, you live in the time of telephones.
Dial a number and wait:
the night bursts, and music appears
for you and only you.
Then you're annoyed —
they've standardized you,
and you understand
that there's no one to complain to.

   3.
Indeed,
they've made you of steel.
If I shoot you from too close —
the bullets will ricochet at me.

Who of us is the nation —
you or me?
The voice of a nation is the voice of God.
Who dares to say
that we are one.
The sharpshooter and the target,
The target and the sharpshooter.

Gaze at the road
between you and me.
Let us burn in tranquility.[5]

  4.

The airplane will lift you
and you will sense tears on your cheeks.
The earth left from beneath your feet,
and to you it seems
that life passed alongside you.
Turn it back
and suddenly you will understand,
that this already happened.
This melody once reigned over you,
this plain was barren,
and a mist above the path
fell in light stripes.
Your nation awaited you:
and the one who played on the square
awaited you,
and the wounded, before a field of gallows,
awaited you,
and the brave, and the proud, and the beautiful,
with swords in blood
they awaited you.

---

5 Several possibilities exist here in the translation. The poet may have in mind "myr," which can be translated as peace, tranquility, or the world. Or he may have in mind "myro" (myrrh or holy oil). The prepositional case ending allows for this ambiguity.

But you passed by,
and suddenly the eyes of many
are looking at your back.
You squint,
but I cannot help you.
The plane will lift you,
and you will stand abreast with the distance
and will be miserably small.

This is our music.

    5.
Music comes suddenly:
barriers are shattered and sounds fall,
like parachutists from the night sky.
The silk snapped,
threads of a swing stretched,
and tracers of bullets cut into the sleepy city.
You, too, tug the ring,
and it carries you beyond the wind,
like a torn page from a notebook.
You think this is a dream,
but when the city below comes alive
and begins to strike up to greet you,
it becomes painful for you.
You come to your senses
in one of the rooms
of a tall paneled building.
You are lost.
Your love sleeps, bundled
                          in a blanket,

she's still just a child.
You look for a cigarette with trembling fingers,
and the match leads you out of the darkness.
You turn off the radio,
open up the window and see
how buds of parachutes explode in the sky.
The sounds wash away:
another moment —
and you flare up like a bulb
that they've screwed into a socket.

A STORMY SEASON

I.
In evening twilight
when the sheer silhouettes of marlets
slash the autumn sky,
in the deep and quiet city
we began our love
like a revolution.

The day of our passion
is here, among these neighborhoods,
whose age-old cobblestones
are flooded with the shadows of bare trees:
your involuntary gaze
touched them,
and the wind,
tearing off this mask of calm,
unfurled us like a flag.

The darkness fell, the city
all around breathed lights.

O golden sorrow of the Slavs,
the thirst of justice uplifts us,
red and black shadows –
a field of fire,
from which we emerged,
each sure of himself.
The first lines of the dawn
paint the heart of the republic
that beats
in the industrial parts of the city.

2.
O nation, I am a part of you
and perceive your strength:
like a weary beast
the city breathes in the evening.

We have paid dearly for everything.

The history of the nation – is our history,
the history of the country – is our history,
we have written it ourselves:
in the black contour of the city
flashes of our hearts –
the ferocious eyes of a bull.

"We won't give our victory to anyone,"
the boys are laughing.
We have obstinate blood,
and in the word
dives: Strike.

3.
The suburbs are covered with snow.

Trains float out of the fog,
honey-colored, milky, scorching,
trains gravitate toward the city
that reddens like a dark flame
in the white show.

Invisibly space fills
in sounds and colors,
the light silhouettes of buildings,
like sculpted maple leaves
float in the cold wine.

In the quite wintry world,
the golden, graceful, proud
city,

that conscious of its greatness
shines in fantastic colors.

You will be great, o nation,
that carries your capital
like a defenseless child in your arms.

      4.
People are in sweaters.

In the evenings they fill up the city:
agitated northern characters,
ordinary in your problems,
great in your solidarity.
Trolley buses swim in the trampled snow,
in waves of streetlamps and advertisements,
trolley buses with frozen windows,
shining and bubbly,
people exit and enter,
they want to come to an understanding with the world:
today this is an icy palace,
filled with sparkles
and the warmth of human bustle.

People in sweaters,
who gave back the day to the flow of a river,
now, right after work,
hands in their pockets,
eyes, quick and lustrous,
gaze, weigh,
    want to notice everything
this trampled snow,
cars in snowdrifts,
the yard of a factory

and ringing voices
that in the frosty wind
sway the light of projectors.
It is quiet for them in this world.

This is their world,
and in it they are great.

5.

This garden in the mountains –
light and tall, in snow –
are cut with paths.

Today this garden is empty.
We – are in it,
we fill it with ourselves.
The unsteady light of the mountain ash –
red and white,
we walk between the snowdrifts.

The city – is below,
cutters, chiseled
from ice
lie at their moorings.
The city – as though on your palm
lives with its affairs,
woven from lights and fog.

The grove above Vydubichy
is a Varangian queen
in Slavic furs.

THE CATHEDRAL

A cycle

    I.
When the sun sets
the pine trees float
in red and black waves,
tall, slim, golden,
like will-o'-the-wisps around the city.

Drowning in these whimsical shadows
we take the path strewn with pine needles.
I love you:
in this translucent aromatic vault of trees
we become solemn and reserved.

The harsh dusk of oak trees and the maples
of distant crystalline years:
acorns fall in rays of sun,
carving out bays, stations, ports,
we are behind them
entering into hugs, into arguments, into the unknown,
into a whimsical world
with the aroma of blood and milk,
and above all this —like total forgiveness —
the austere light of the oak trees and maples.
O, blue cars of the metro
that will take us to the park of your childhood:
dusk and silence,
in the darkness
we crossed the river Dnipró
and, embracing,
set off on the path between the pines
to your building.

2.
Bees fly.

Bees wrap us,
in their thick honey
a world of wooden vessels,
a world of buildings, bridges and hills
floats with the ringing voices of children.

My world in the shadow of trees.
My king,
with velvet, with boats, with maidens,
you return in the delicate waves —
the ringing city
has covered up its head in lament:
there beyond the hills birds have shrouded
your regiment with their wings.

We open the window, the day
lies down like silk
onto the hills of the right bank:
the rails of the metro in the snow go off
beyond the horizon.

The branchy trees of Vidradny,
whose name means joy,
the sweet snowstorm of Vidradny —
a dove-cote
for all kinds —
raven-black, hazel ones, and simply a dove-cote:
arrows fly,
and arrows hit with precision —
in the transparent pine air of the left bank,
like a brass sword, you fly up in my arms,
covered with a glow,
steep.

3.
The city is in cigarette smoke —completely industrial,
in smoke at sunrise
we —are in blood, we are young riders,
we come on horseback,
and in the grass above us like turtle-doves,
young maidens, beautiful and tender,
and loved, for they
are in the smoke of sunrise.

The eyes of the god of grasses,
those green, joyful, entreating
eyes of our spouses
that still both entreat and caress —
at dawn,
in flight they caught us,
they still are carrying out wine
to the blue-eyed, fair-haired and young.

The city breathes, the hills are
in a blue glow,
the sky in gold,
the maidens in furs,
this headlong gallop rises up, carries off and sways:
O silky grass of the town of Berestechko
and the strike of the cavalry at Batizhok.

4.
A nest of eagles.
The steps lead upward,
the branches of trees above them
create a resilient arch,
in their shadow
the bronze of sabers darkens with blood.

We interlock the bronze of our shields,
our faces cannot be seen,
we see —everything:

arrows ring bouncing off our shields,
they fall into the dust cloud on the steps.

A tree of arrows —
black, heavy, stifling,
like the braids of Byzantine women slaves.
Resilient, like a lynx, our flag
crawls upward,
avoiding the surly arrows.
The fur of the lynx

smells of the early morning forest,
the eyes of the lynx
are ablaze like blue fire.
we raise our taut bows,
the ringing forest arrows hum
like wild bees
through the green braiding of branches.

Having thrown our shields onto our shoulders
we walk upward,
wiping off our sabers as we walk.
The world in the valley
is clear,
and there is glory
for the victors.

5.
Dusk beyond the towers —
we
walk onward from the time of our youth:
I barely recognize
old friends —
something else unites us today.

Oh endless file
of an eternal *rzeczpospolita*[6] movement:
the reserved rustling of words,
untouched snow on the towers
and in the harsh light
the beautiful faces of princesses.

The Universe is above us —
like the shadow of a snowfall, but
on a continent covered with snow
someone builds a home,
someone will establish himself.
In the center of the Universe —
there is a planet of people,
this steel and cruel world,
this beautiful world,
worthy
of living in.

---

[6] The Polish word for "republic."

BENEATH THE BRIGHT SUN

SONG TO THE SUN

The air light,
Ashes light,
as well as traces
          of fires:
Water in the fire,
in the fire —a horde,
and a red sky
on the horizon.

(Three princes came,
three swords to the side —
three falcons in the heavens)
          Dazhboh[7]
(They burned smoke,
they mustered houses —
the princes marshaled us to battle)
          Dazhboh

The air light,
Ashes light,
as well as traces
          of fires:
Water in the fire,
in the fire —a horde,
and a red sky
on the horizon.

---

[7] The ancient Slavic sun god.

ARIAS

A Cycle

1.
When white lambs of clouds
roll in a disorderly herd to the east,
we go to meet the sun,
resonant from the heat and stone dust
that remains in the folds of our clothes.

The cold water of a waterfall
smolders beneath the hooves of horses,
like a cluster of grapes
the evening sun
hangs above the battlements of yellow brick towers,
and the wind in perfume fills
light canvas tents
on the silent square of the City,
and in alleys illuminated by the moon,
women slowly emerge from tight bikini briefs
and slowing their white thighs,
with hot white legs
they strive to capture the boundless night,
pleating them with us behind our back.

And if we come as eternal horsemen,
we will grow
and strengthen our freedom to the East

2.
At that hour,
as in the red mountains,
where a powerful dove-colored bush
surrounds clear springs,
we begin to dream of Slavic stars,
we douse our bonfires
with animal skin buckets

that gleam between cliffs
like diamonds in a chest,
and the muzzles of our horses
begin to look to the west.

When at last
we climb off our saddles
women with stomachs steaming white
press up to our darkened faces
and throw their naked and desirous bodies
into our arms.

    3.

The women —white, soft and wet
alongside the black stones of beaten roads
with warm pink breasts
and strong moist thighs —
jostle our shoulders, stomachs, and knees.

And much much later
when the echo of our proud songs quiets
near a falling dust-cloud on the path,
with thrown open legs the women
hold our pressed contours
on their bodies.

FAR AWAY

A Cycle

1.

Cows walk across the sun,
and from a golden lion
they have –
gold-bearing eyes
and golden milk.

Warriors in sharp helmets
listen to the brass song,
taut bows on their shoulders
like the bent horns of bulls.
A bumblebee flies

like a snake,
a calf begins to trundle
like a pea-sized muscle man.[8]

And hollyhocks bloom
as though they were painted

2.

There were stiff trees,
and hazy nights,
the evening star
hushed:
wise men passed –
they stopped
other princes passed –
they stopped:

---

8   Literally "Kotyhoroshko" from Ukrainian fairytales. He is a tiny boy born from a pea plant who has incredible strength and defends his parents and others from evil.

and a trumpet[9] trumpets
and keeps playing

3.
You walk through the garden standing

Voices float away
and just boats
direct their sharp noses
toward the crimson of the sky
and the blue flocks of waves

The ruins of Troy are still smoking:
be joyful, beautiful one,
your prince is sailing,
all in a golden glow

Clear smoke
in the distance

4.
The summer, warmth and summerwarmth –
how much time already
has flowed away,
how much in a star, at dawn,
has been taken from a shoulder,
in flight

July and for the linden trees –
splendorous,
but will it be splendorous, brothers,
for us to stand leaning on our swords
shoulder to shoulder on the river Don

My Cossack units are jumping –
dust, blood and wounds –

---

9   Literally a *surma*, a Ukrainian instrument of the horn family.

whores are crying in the towers –
my Kursk regiment is jumping
Our wish is fulfilled –

Not to be deprived of freedom:
there where a turtle dove is cooing,
my Kursk regiment is jumping
through the millennium

5.
Apple trees – super white
a wide white world – super white –
as you ride across the field,
through the field,
in white

Slowly— across the field,
like a peacock, through the field – a lily,
a snowy lily

6.
It will be mysticism and smoke
heavy and gray
that fly over us
like stretched out flocks
like an eternal young snake

And further there will be reality and dreams
that will begin to rock
all of them,
they will enter more and more silently
and cut off the garrison

Afterward there will be shadow and a garden
and the gold of the sun
and glory
and the maidens will have– sheer veils,
and no path back

AN ADVENTURE

1.

Herds went to forage,
no longer herds, but dust,
and where there was dust –
there's snow today

The horses set off in a slow gait –
your breasts opened up –
two small buds, two tiny little boats,
two dainty morsels,
but all the same –
there's snow today

Hawks set off along the ravine –
homesickness began to overcome me,
your eyes arrows to me –
two blue lambs,
saying:

"There's snow today"

2.

Queen-princess –
first tender, then threatening
O, Div Lada—[10]
it's snowing

The queen squints –
her breasts like stone walls
O, Div Lada –
it's snowing

---

10   Div is the name of the chief god in the ancient Slavic pantheon. Lada is the ancient Slavic goddess of love and beauty.

Boys like faithful lions
near the queen

O, Div Lada –
it's snowing

And from that princess
just snow to the knees
O, Div Lada –
blood will start flowing

3.
I will go out onto the mountain for a walk,
I will go out to whistle,
I will go out to call together my band:

– We need high walls brothers,
we need to chase away the threatening army,
we need to tear off some clothes
to taste the sweet apple,
because our flocks have already left to forage

and our horses have set off in a slow gait,
and the hawks have set off along the ravine.

THE SHIPSAILING SONG

A Cycle

A soft starry breeze
                of all
                              the earth's
                                            waterfalls
Wandered in the rain,
                searching
                                            and crying.
The bay in fog
                as though in gold
                                            and the ships
set off to unknown lands,
                as though they melt,
                                  extinguishing
                                            themselves,
A summer of water
                in the translucent beams
                                  of arms.
A summer of these princesses
                      goes further
                                      through the reflection
of dandelions.
                Everything passes,
                                  and again
all begins
                with the bay,
                          the fog
                                  and ships.
O ship builders!
                Plunge
                          a ringing
                              saw
into the heart of trees,
                heavy,

                              soft,
                                        and hot,
like the breasts of
                    pregnant
                                young
                                          Varangian princesses
who fall asleep at dawn
                    and see
                                unknown
                                          dreams.
O ship builders...
Like freshly made wine,
                    let us pour
                                our
                                          ship
into the translucent chalice
                    of these
                                riggings
                                          in pine-tree gold,
that, like honey,
                    flows
                                from the wounds
                                          of trees
into the ringing of axes,
                    into the bustling of carpenters
and the heavy
                    blows
                                of hammers.
O ship builders...
You and the fortress —
                    that is all.
The stone of the fortress in the grass —
                                like a wasp
                                          in amber.
All
      is in the pouring out of sabers,
                                and a wave of amber
                                          carries

ships into a summer of palms —
                        unearthly,
                              mad,
                                              and bright.

2.
Where the blooming lilac
               in violet
                          shadows
                                           pours out
onto bodies of those spread out,
               sleepy
                          and bright
                                        in the grass.
Where everything remained high,
               for everything
                            will be ground
                                           up:
the scent of flour,
        a soft translucent breeze
                                           and ships.
The reflection of sun
          in the binding
                      air
                               flows,
as the multi-colored capes of horsemen
                         melt
                            in the slow
                                               trail of
a dust-cloud,
and with a slow gesture of a hand
                         the steel of an ax
                                   enters
                                           the golden
                                                 wood
and emerges from it —
               damp,
                       heavy,
                             covered with soot.

Everything —is to come,
                    and everything —
                                    is created
                                            in this century.
Just bodies spread out
                in love,
                        in the grass,
                                    half-asleep:
on the rocky shore —
                reflections of the sun
                                in strawberry
                                            droplets —
the meeting
        of steel and wood —
in a translucent ray
                the transparent drone of a bee.
His captive woman
                and princess
                            for whom he awaits
is in this land,
where only one thing lives,
                    swirls,
                                and cries:
the shipbuilder's song;
where with the resilient blood of a tree
                        well-watered are the cables,
                                    stones
                                            and the earth,
just like their last
            bread,
                    so longed for
                                yet so bitter,
you touch to your lips
your captive maid,
            the princess.
The first droplets of rain.
                    Silver
                            and silk

                                       awaken us,
    wrapping around our bodies
                        and pulling them close,
                                savage,
                                        and supple
    like the hissing of a snake.

    Sounds interweave
                        and bits of thoughts
    into the sonorous view
                        of the shipbuilder's song,
                                  of love,
                                      and a deluge.

            3.
You will come in the spring.
                      From the azure
                                blue
                                        dwelling places
smoke will curl,
        and slanting
                arrows
                        will fall on them,
and through black padlocks,
                like a beast,
                          the ship
                                will crawl
and will strike its breast
        to the painted
                gate
                        of the dock.
Still to curse
        the painted gate
                with a strange
                        courageous
                                    sketch,
like an unfinished ornament
                of destiny,
                      of love,

                                                    and death:
on dusty towers
            surmas[11]
                        sadly shout,
and in this shout —
                        we are naked.
                                        Naked
                                                and relentless.
And the ship will crawl out.
                        And will strike its breast.
                                                    Then look
for our people
            in all
                        the uncountable
                                    shelters
                                                and taverns.
The kingdom will fall,
                the end of the
                                mannered
                                                grandeur,
and the world will turn
                for our
                        hordes
                                long and without purpose.
You will come in the spring,
                    in a white dust-cloud,
                                    all white
                                                and gold
from such alien
            beliefs,
                        and fancies,
                                    and everyday life,
and you will see:
            on the horizon

---

11   A native Ukrainian folk instrument related to the horn family. The *surma* was often used as a call to battle, a call to a gathering, and as part of the funeral service.

    black specks
               of ships,
like eyes,
     having opened
              they look,
                         and are present.

       4.
Cliffs fall above the shore,
                   droplets
                      color
                            the backdrop
in the crimson of sabers.
And red shields
      hooked to the knee,
                     like a flower, lay
along both rows,
where true gold
was felled.

The cliffs fall above the shore,
                   from black forests
a whirlpool of black dogs,
          and wolves,
                         and axes,
a dragon rises,

       and his scales blaze,
and in shaggy waves
the fairy tale begins.

And the herd flows.
And on the dark pilings of bridges
they pull out something from beneath cloaks,
and the night turns bloody,
and bleached iron collars
whiten in the fog
         in gold
                  and silver.
See off your guests.
The vessels sail off
to the Norwegian seas.

THE MIDDLE AGES

A Cycle

1.

The third estate is
skunk drunk.
Rain dances
like a hetman [in a funk].
It keeps on embroidering
black and white towers in trickling drips.
Dingy glasses
on the tables –
the world swaying
in your eyes.
The velvet of swords get wet,
slingshots and the more the better,
and it rings like crystal,
a ring of raspberry
hollyhocks.

2. HEADBANGERS

The sky –
        above us,
below us –
        cobblestones,
our steps –
        quick and tender.
And from the touch
        of our hands
iron catches fire.
Our lips –
    total
        thirst,
our hearts –
        hunger,
and it makes no difference
who is friend,

                         and who
             is foe.
        Hey, everybody around us!
        Raise up
                  the goblets
        to drink to our heads!

3. A LANDSCAPE

Night,
everything is floating,
just the moon
and white smoke in the valleys

(roses – red – shadows)
everything shimmers and melts
the blue glow of lines
and the scent of broad-leafed lilies
spread out along the valleys.

4. BARBARIANS

Here,
    in the boundless,
                hostile spaces,
stubbornly,
    slowly
            and gradually
we will vanquish
            all
                to our word,
setting it
    with the highest
                law.
Until the white
            river
                swings,
In silence we

        come together
                chest to chest,
the spring sun
      will
          glow
in our eyes
    pale
         from ferocity.
The rain will wash away
             footprints
                   after the exiles,
the rain washes away
         days
             and years –
we will pass
     through harsh paths,
moved
   at the command
            of a hand.
Snow will fall,
      and a mighty
              formation
will float out
     from the horizons
               of our contours –
be blessed
   and conquered,
world,
   azure
     and gold.

5. WOE IS ME

Before us –
     light-colored Taurida[12]

---

[12] The old name for the Crimea, which comes from the Greek name for the indigenous inhabitants, the Tauri.

and behind us –
        Taurida
above us there is –
smoke and fog
we plait the manes
              for the cremelos
we plait the manes
              for the bays
we plait the manes for the tiny fireflies
...and the young
        Hungarian steeds
walk
    in burning Taurida
young
        Hungarian riders
and their reddish
              sun.

6. A CHEERFUL JOURNEY

    A marble
even sad
beautiful girl
      walks through the steppe,

and together with her –
a silver jingling
along with three squadrons in gold.

On the young girl – not a thread,
the young girl is like a swan:
      she walks about prancing
festively
      barking the camp's orders.
And the three squadrons in gold
      roll off in every direction
like beads.

A CARAVAN

A Cycle

1.
West – East.
East – West.
Wheels knock on the tracks,
unfamiliar plains, covered
with dust,
where sleepy turtle-doves
and indecipherable signs
on the stations.
We pass them in a rush,
through the windows of the rail cars
remembering the names,
Great Handel!
Pillow cases – for the camera,
zinc buckets – for the eletronics.
A pack of wolves
rushed through Budapest.
Greetings, Europe!
Rock and roll – a *kazachok*.[13]
Rock and roll – a *kazachok*.
And the bust
of a naked slut.
Look out, customs,
Tsarist Scythia is *on the move*!

2.
There is a raven over Serbia.

The great movement of peoples
circumvents Bosnia and Croatia,
Serbia
drowns in splendor.

---

[13] A lively traditional Ukrainian dance.

The Islamic-Slavic south:
a Moor girl on a bar sign
elegantly takes off her underwear.
Right behind the horde of fair-haired barbarians
go the carts with dinars:
through the dust of three countries
the path of the caravan
goes to the south.
A-a-ay!
Bachisara-ai![14]
Like Stenka Razin[15]
at a Persian princess,
an iron knot
falls on Serbia like a hawk –
a new capital on the crossroads of paths.

3.
Through the Balkan spring
along a really narrow street from the train station
floats a wave of an early morning train.
In the sunny dust
Serbs on bicycles
chase the endless stream
of the Great Handel.
The burning heat of the economic crisis
      roused tribes from the distant North.
"Hey, La-da-ga,[16] my homeland La-da-ga!"
Golden Rus
floats into the bazaar
on Novgorodian boats.

---

14   Situated in Crimea and the location of the famous fountain described in Pushkin's long poem "The Fountain of Bachisarai."

15   The famous Don Cossack, who fomented rebellion against the Tsarist Russian government in the late 1660s until his capture and execution in 1671. The marauder garnered considerable popular support and became a folk hero in Russia.

16   Old Ladoga is an historic Russian village not far from the city of Kirovsk.

4.
A farewell coffee
with a Serbian family.
The din of the bazaar doesn't waft
to the mansard under the roof.
I'm already lighting up my gazillionth cigarette:
a dark thick liquid
in the clay cup
snakelike strands of the steam
coils like a dancer's
torso.

The last dinars –
on souvenirs:
the liquor of the Great Handel
foams in my blood.

The snows of a boundless country
from sea to sea
will be sown in wrappers
of Yugoslavian candies.

In the golden whirlwind
the empire drowns on wheels.

5.
The legendary commuter train
flies through the night
from Subotnytsia to Chop.
A great silk path.
Yugoslavia – California,
California – Yugoslavia:
on wagons
through the desert –
for California gold.
The cigarette smoke dissipates
beneath the ceiling,
like dust whipped up

following cowboy Joe.
Hey, commuter train!
Hey, hey, commuter train!
Silver jangling of wheels
ro-ro-rolled
through three countries
in your train cars,
watered
with the fragrances of blood,
cognac
and an excess of profits.

EVENINGS. TWILIGHT. IMPRESSIONS.

PRELUDE

The beautiful hands of lovers
slowly will come through evening lights
and, as if a barely audible sigh,
will touch me in silence.

And, perhaps, I will buy my way out right after spring
for so inappropriately
loving those slender shoulders
and the bright faces of my darlings.

For winter anxiously
painting silhouettes on the glass
and palms beckoning for great
snows.

JOURNEYS

Silver bells ring beautifully,
dark night calls to journeys,
the knocking of commuter trains
along illuminated platforms.

A warm wind blows from the south.
How will you still toss out your summons to fate?
For a small reddish poni
I would give up everything in the world.

Coals glow reddishly,
the river – is like the sap of a maple,
and—the anxious breath of a miracle.

Black sand-willows have risen.
Like a knife into white breasts,
silver oars beat into the water.

A GOLD-BEARING SONNET
(IN OLD KYIV)

In the silence of these placid alleys
with just the sun shining on the windows
and the nearly unnoticeable echo
of footsteps — like the purring of a kitten.

The mannered weary fancy of April,
rooftops — light as kisses,
and laughter echoing sonorously
in the azure tents of space.

Embers slowly disappear,
all is the gold of transformations
and the pliancy of silver flashes
in the translucent chalice of the basin.

It is just music drowning
in the melancholy walls of the yard.

IN THE SOUTH

A room, a table, as well as an ashtray,
a not quite finished cigarette,
a small electric lamp
traces a circle of thoughts.

A window out to the garden, a black cat
that rolls the ball of the moon,
and walls have the scent of lilacs
and a southern star falls.

An old building with a mezzanine
and a velvety season —
it's a little sad, a little sweet.

And above it all, like a dream,
a happy melody resounds
with a mocking bird — in unison.

A MAGIC ACT

Just half-shadows, halftones and snow
that fell and froze on eyelashes,
it trampled bright colors, blustered,
enchanted this night, without quieting down.

Into every sleepy Kyivan courtyard
it brought the unease and sorrow of the roads,
like a puppy spinning around hurriedly
it tore off high-voltage wires.

Alcohol and smoke saved us,
in a circle like gypsies we conned
the "Campfire," that was wet, like a gray pilgrim.

And the card dealt each his destiny,
and only a few minutes remained
to understand the mystery of the theater.

THE LAST APPRENTICE OF MAGISTER KNECHT[17]

He, who stepped out onto the mountain along the steep path,
who stands beneath the rain like a sinner,
who walked like a prophetic oracle
along this forgotten way in solitude.

How many upward flights there have been,
victories and falls, and all this is just so
to look today at a freight car quietly rattling
in the rust-colored valley.

He leaned a cheek against the rough bark
of these pine trees. And – no tears, no resentment.
Just – peace, as though the water on the window
were washing away the mountain landscapes.

...It grew dark and he took in
the solemnity of the silent evening.

He left just the slow falling
of pine needles behind.

---

17   The hero of Hesse's novel *The Glass Bead Game* Joseph Knecht.

BATTLE

A southern wind completely powders
buskins and capes, swords and slings,
blending the rows, and whispered suddenly
to the centurions about awful disaster.

And along the silence of olive meadows
where the paths are tangled like galley riggings,
a tent swayed a crimson shadow
and enveloped the glow of doused campfires.

The frugal Huns began to move about,
the call to war of the Nubians grew quiet,
and they fought silently, fiercely without thinking,

and already when bloody battle had been raised
on the earthen ramparts and there was no hope for salvation –
the cold heavy night fell.

THE MIRAGE

Everything grows foggy in this dream
where fairies pass barefoot,
Achean sacrifices smolder,
and bronze shields glisten.
Everything grows foggy in this dream.

The azure marble of Chersonesus,
the branchy shadows of long rows
where they fell like the transparent train of a dress,
and above the black bay
the azure marble of Chersonesus shines.

The slow-moving grace of shapely
terracotta goddesses. And there
melts away in the distant smoke an ataman,
who in the muddy backwater
of Slavdom placed pantheons
of shapely terracotta goddesses.

IMPROVISATION

Let's rush off to Debreczen[18]
to that tavern Liszt used to go to.
You're fall in love, certainly,
with the slight dusk of the land of Artemis.

There on a sultry day near churches
age-old Bosorkan[19] witches
will tell legends
of blood, robberies and love.

The moon will look down sadly,
and the night will sway reveries,
as though Attila the Hunn
had sent it again to shake up Byzantium.

But we have rain, fog and autumn,
neither a cart or money, no matter!
Let's forget things for a bit,
let's rush off to Debreczen.

---

18   One of the largest towns in Hungary outside of the capital of Budapest.
19   The Borsokan are ugly old witches out of Hungarian folklore who have the ability to transform into various animals.

SPANISH MELODIES

The night, cicadas, love and a jasmine bloom.
Caravels stir into a campaign.
Cortez is taking three hundred
of the best Spanish blades with him.

(Ah, Castile – port at night,
black eyes and white sabers
and Madonnas with three burning candles).

Brazen adventurer or god –
no one will never now learn.
Simply three hundred of the best swords –
to the shoulder – a shoulder – and a full house.

(Ah, Castile – the lament of guitars,
the queen's shawl falls –
and Toledo's direct blow).

the first safety anchors that are thrown into the quiet surf
like sailors at the breasts of sluts.
And let the myth remain:
of Montezuma, Cortez, the campaign.

(Ah, Castile – port at night,
black eyes and white sabers
and Madonnas with three burning candles).

JOAN OF ARC

The annoying rain keeps hammering.
The last hope is the steel of a saber.
France is breathing
through your lips now, Joan.

For victory, Joan,
your eyes are focused deep.
And in France the twelth regiment
is tying up all the roads.

Joan. They couldn't manage. It's too late.
The company's in a gallop. To reach the final, and not their end.
Albion, Orleans and a maiden –
are all interwoven. We won't sort it out.

THE SEASONS ON ST. ANDREW'S DESCENT[20]

1. WINTER

Grow, my gang brothers, like the grass –
everything is unreachable and fantastic,
then we'll will start up a Waterloo rumble
so they don't let us down.

Sweep away, wind, and in the alcoves
young girls plait house brooms,
for winter is still turning the window-panes
silver in the playful alleys.

All day in a light half-dream
fires flash in pipes
and fade away on faces.

And from chimneys a dry,
crackling pine smoke is sown
with the barely noticeable scent of pitch.

2. SPRING

When fog swirls through the alleyways
and hangs in the carved attics,
from fragrant firewood a lit fire
warms our hands with a slight flame.

And we remake history of the Slavs,
where there will be Div and the prince's keeper of the castle,
and the steward of the golden gates,
and the squeaking of carts, damaged during the march.

---

20   One of the most famous streets in Kyiv that starts in the Podil section of the city near the Dnipro River that goes up to St. Andrew's Cathedral at the top to the older part of the city. It is lined largely by art studios, galleries and cafes. Vendors also sell their wares to tourists on the sidewalk.

The regiments returned and drank up the wine
in silver cups to toast all who had lain down in battle.
It's already becoming dusk. The city, like a light wreath,
is swaying on the green current.

And the chilled haunches of blackish prisoners
shine dully through transparent silk.

3. SUMMER

Bumble bees, retro style, Podil.
Spin it with breathing because it's a holiday,
we're hired to play the hurdy-gurdy
of distant days.

The quatrain's script – so motley.
The pubs are buzzing, and a swarm
of legends streams about the castle and whores,
a pastoral of the sixties.

Sic transit glori…[21] For the customers
a violin screeching, in discord
bands of sparrows scurry.

So raise up your full tankards
and strike your spread hands on the table
for Esmeralda's white goat.

4. AUTUMN

At midnight fair-haired girls
open greenish windows—
rain came and strum
like noisy whistling arrows.

An unsteady shadow floats above us,
wrapping necks in scarves,

---

21   Meaning: glory like this fades.

we enamel smoky Kyiv
and the crimson flashes of lights.

Everything already is so close and unsure –
these violet flashes
and swirling in unison,

and in the silver dusk of the alcoves
mysterious lines interweave
lavish, Baroque beauties.

THE WINTER OF OUR CITY

1. A POEM INSTEAD OF A DEDICATION

There are no sad love affairs,
just from time to time
if you walk for a while through snow-covered streets,
you remember old fairytales.

We were together so little
that it seems an entire eternity pass
and that is why this is:
For you.

2.

Give me your hand – and we'll go
through the streets of Old Kyiv,
because it's just in winter when
hands seek hands so fervently.

Give me your hand – and we will go
past the hair salons and stores
because just in winter our breath
freezes this way on glass.

We'll chew on nuts
and Christmas mandarins
and we'll talk happily
about everything, just not about love,

let the colored snow fall,
like the ribbons of a serpentine,
in the neighborhoods of Old Kyiv
onto the tiled roofs.

An ancient Slavic fairytale
about steeds covered up in snow,
loaded catapults
and stares from embrasures.

Give me your hand – and we will go
through the wintry silence of Kyiv
in the sweet-talk of distant recollections
and blue snowstorms.

    3.
If you want, I'll tell you
one simply secret
about how snow falls
slowly and quietly at night

and how the Polovtsian invader
looked at a branch of the yevshan herb,
and then long and wildly
an echo died down in the distance,

and the enraged Ihor
was returning along
Borychev Descent, and bells tolled,
like arrows hitting red shields.

And if you want, I'll tell you about
how our guys forced the enemy
into a dead end of narrow streets
with shots from the rooftops.

Let's chat a bit
about poems, about the snow and legends –
for, you know, this, perhaps, is the last time
the snow is falling so quietly.

    4.
Surely we soon will forget
distant fairytales and will go out
into the night so unnoticeably
as the light falls from the windows

and so, as though beneath black towers,
the first queues of the inhabitants of Rus
tied their belts to one other,
wandering up to their knees in snow,

and the riders divided up
in their blue silk capes,
and foreign flags appeared dimly
with Christmas banners

We'll grab a taxi somewhere,
and in the velvet silence
our lips will be chilled easily and become light,
like the snow on streetlamps,

and in buildings with chimeras
spectres will peacefully drink
fragrant Indian tea
from English porcelain

5. A POEM INSTEAD OF AN EPILOGUE
While the snow is falling,
sad dragons on the buildings
will remember us,
for not only Richard[22]
thrust his way to Kyiv
to build a castle and leave,
and we remain here
forever.

---

22   The castle of Richard the Lionhearted at 15, St. Andrew's Descent. Richard never set foot in the city, but the building was given the name by the local residents.

THE END OF A GLOOMY DAY

Hey, autumn, bells made of tin-plate –
rain awakens the rooftops,
cars scurry at the intersections,
and in the yards yardsmen
rake yellow leaves into piles
and already are putting matches up close,
and the white smoke is like a song.

And in the evening when the asphalt
glistens like mother of pearl,
in the motley mixture of coats,
the umbrellas, like storks,
grow still on one leg
and sad lights twinkle.

In the rain, in the fog, these melodic
sparklings of bright lines
lay down along and through them

everything – more cryptic and closer,
and the look of a woman mysteriously
touches your eyes

CIRCULATION
(IN OLD KYIV)

The starry night is like a filled goblet,
and the outer edges of the city are an eternal mystery.
Swift as shadow Varangian boats
barely flow through the waves of the Pochaina River.

The prince's lip has quite timorous,
Slavic thoughts – darkly black.
At half past noon on a Monday
fair-haired riders mount their steeds.

SAVE OUR SOUL

Hey, Veronika, this is even sad,
and one quick stolen little kiss is burning
somewhere in my soul
and the moon is behind my back.

We, maybe, didn't finish saying something…
And train number 138 started off.
Madonna of the city outskirts,
pray for our souls.

A REALLY BRIGHT DAWN

Whether I loved you, or not –
I don't know, all of this is like a child's dreams,
once again gray days are rolling up
like the melancholy waves of the River Desna.

I came just the way I am,
everything that had to come to pass, came to pass.
Don't reproach me for every bad thing,
because we just argue on these streets.

Ave sol![23]
    Ave sol!
           And let
the cobweb
of these lucid melodies
    drowsily rock us –
and then
    above the ruins of the city
quietly waft to us:
"Hail to the sun!"
The beginning
    of a new
        life.

---

[23] "Hail to the sun" in Latin.

IN A GALLOP BENEATH THE MOON

In nights dark, imperious, wicked,
when it overlows,
you will ask, "Make us
at least our daily bread,
or at least a war."

For everything isn't so, everything isn't good,
for everything – is perfidious and false,
everything also – is thrown in the fire,
let wings grow for others
after us.

For everything is not worth even the half-dawning
haze
and a voice
will still utter:
"Take
a sword that will break this circle."

For whether from the deserts, or from Judea,
there will be a black wave of treachery and slavery,
a rider will jump
and with his sword will carry out
the inextinguishable line.

DIAPHANOUS MORNING

To destroy everything and forget all —
in the bustle, in the rain, in May,
in mid-February to fall in love
with your defenselessness.

Eternity and silence. Doors to the street —
open, and the morning open.
Translucent buildings like beehives
in the interweaving of aromatic lines.

It consists of stasis, whispers, and colors,
and at last from great bridges
it is just the ships casting off

into a white tea-pot whistle.

A RENAISSANCE

A cycle

I.
Byzantium and gloaming –
        early morning,
                like the taste of cowbane,
and the swaying of tile roofs –
        like the silk
           of chariots
              and capes.
Enter this day –
      as if you were
    touching the blade
             of a knife.
Enter an opal room
      with galleries
           of docks and boats.
A little asphalt street
      with a careless
           movement
              will open
the sleepy port
    and the poetry of telegrams,
and on the backdrop of green trees is
           the red
              brick of buildings –
like the thin
   torn goatskin
           of an ancient book.
A white Slavic
     sun
       from a hundred
          commotions
raises this city
    onto towers
        and spears

and across the way paints
                         a light
                                       and a beloved face
either young girls,
               or young ladies,
                             or like –
                                                 a renaissance portrait.

               2.

Noontime, dust,
everything so glaring and austere
that even the water in waterfalls
becomes the color of gold.

(Our passion has already thrown us
into the shade from an umbrella over a small table,
with a view onto Podil
and the foamy chill of glasses).

It's a little sad because
it seems crumpled and excessive
clothes, the city, life,
just the sun – gooey like honey,
teaches all of the defeated
that only what is taken by blood and force
is a delight,
and in the limiting vividness of colors
our words are vivid,
barely silverplated on the outside by dark
love, like a Tartar raid.

               3.

In the evening trucks wash the streets,
and the asphalt becomes velvet,
like the sound of a flute,
and this velvet sound of the evening
spreads above us
like the scent of blossoming cherries.

In the end,
music is like words,
but here –
the echo suddenly simply rolled
from the tram's rattling,
whether the distant whistle of a steamship,
or the careless laughter of those
who have named this city their own,
and were here for just a short amount of time
that they just left the flapping of torn capes,
the scent of wormwood and weary horses
in these walls.

4.

Illuminate hands with a match
in a silent room
and suddenly see the road between the hillocks,
where reddish dust
covers the hooves of horses,
when the green flow of the Dnipro River
slowly carries away the best
from the horseman's history
of our watch towers.

Sense sudden tenderness
toward your wife,
who passed her gaze through a tiny light
somewhere really far away,
with the peaceful assuredness
of all
whom are loved.

5.

Pass through the fire that burned
those who somehow were walking
abreast with you
up to their knees in the morning fog.
Pass through the fire

that made everyone silent
and left a bleakness on everything.

And then,
looking at the faces of loved ones in the distance,
draw the illuminated city at night –
a marble May-bug on your palm.

COFFEE HOUSES

A Cycle

1. THE COFFEE HOUSE ON PARIS COMMUNE STREET

April,
the air resonating, like the clicking of rifle cocks,
and the wind
removes a dust cloud above the asphalt,
like water
foaming beneath green oars.

(This coffee house
is like an arbor in a pine forest,
brightly illuminated by the sun).

To sit down on a window sill,
to place your cup of coffee next to you
and to recollect
the diaphanous streets of Podil,
where tram cars effortlessly stamp on tracks,
riding out of the morning sun
as though they are recounting
how wet from weariness
the boys slowly reloaded their carbines,
the great idea of France
exhorting them on: "Forward, children!"

2. THE COFFEE HOUSE NEAR THE SQUARE WITH CANNONS

Turkish coffee
from long narrow cups —
like the hot image
of red maples
along the street.

The cold rustling of rain beyond the doors
and the sleepy thirst of mid-day in the coffee house,
where there is only a waitress
with the light blue eyes
of a Polovetsian princess.

3. THE COFFEE HOUSE ON THE CORNER OF SAKSAHANSKY STREET

To stick your hands into the pockets of your leather jacket
and to look at your customers,
hewn in the gloom
from the colors of leaves
and stone.

On a marble-colored table —
the bright ring from a lamp
and a tart
autumn, like a lonely train station
in the mountains.

4. A CUP OF COFFEE AT THE TRAIN STATION

The light of a headlamp
on black cross-ties.

Through the frozen pane one can see
how slowly
the snow is sown
in the pale light of the head-lamp.

5. ON THE ROAD

To warm up your hands with a cup of coffee
and, breathing in its bitter scent,
you understand:
spring will soon be here.

In the town covered with snow —
like a string of wolf tracks —

the black track for a commuter train.
What brought you to these parts?

Like a young animal
you shake off your weariness
and step out into the night
with the sparkling snow,
with the distant voices of hunters
and the crunching sound of fresh blood on their teeth.

THE ARCHIPENKO SCULPTURE

and the heavy visibility of objects
created by us,
we brought them from the place
where we make the world conscious,
not as boundless loneliness
in the surroundings of silence, but as
silhouettes of buildings
in a violet evening and, perhaps,
contours of trees
cleansed by the rain and wind.

...and now
we will leave
an unsteady marble silhouette
of two lovers
in the distance,
marking not our aim
with this,
but simply the purpose of our existence amid the stars,
that with lonely light resemble
sparks of laughter
in greenish Slavic eyes.

REVERIES

A Cycle

1. AN INCOMPREHENSIBLE MIRAGE

The boundlessness of this distance
that touched our eyes is ephemeral,
like the memory of lips turning pale,
and you have to pass through the cold of these wastelands
where everyone's defeat
is like an expensive ruby
                       in the iron shell of a helmet.
And because
this tribute of red tones has to be paid,
and all will pass,
even the warm stone of temples
that thirstily raised their faces
disappearing in black sands.
And then, on the boundary, something long forgotten will approach,
something like laughter or crying
or simply the distant moon
of silver sounds
that quietly falls in the distance.

2. ON A SULLEN STREET

The other side of the snows begins there,
where valleys can barely be seen
with thin rails going off in the depth, but here —
like the watercolor of an unknown master —
the starkness of spires
that reach the sky in loneliness
through the cold light of yellowed winter.

Because of this
you have to silently enter into the swaying of the air
on dark and wet streets,
where the doors of entryways are colored

                                        with rusty paint,
and stains on the walls
are only a sign of the passing centuries,
and don't seek the other side,
but the shortest moment,
for only the doves,
fearfully flying out of the windows of garrets,
can learn every bend
of the tiled sea beneath their wings.

3. A REVERIE OF SPRING

Because the day becomes all the more transparent,
the snow, like a sparkling prophet,
remakes this transparency
into the light melody of rooftops
that, like streaks of colored smoke,
rise up from Podil.[24]

Reserved splashes of bright tones —
in the perfected clarity
of this stone Slavic city,
where the stone — is thin and transparent
                    like branches of trees,
and only toward evening
a light frost, barely streaming,
delicate, like glass,
paints a clumsy sketch of love,
when feelings are still foggy and strange,
and, as though through a veil,
the street passes in rows of green buildings
that rise upward, covered with moss.

4. A PATRIOTIC REVERIE

Autumn arrived,
like a slow night tram
foreboding death,

---

[24] One of the oldest, low-lying parts of the city of Kyiv near the river Dnipró.

it rang with the falling of red leaves
                         beneath feet,
and I called your name Ukraine,
for someone had to
love this land so mightily,
in order to call it
just love.

And all that I had
that I barely glanced through, like a darkened castle
in curtains of rain,
diminished, and suddenly
morning fog
wrapped the alleys all the way to the cornices of buildings,
hiding from sight
the leaves that fell
and the zinc buckets of trash,
and damp cars, covered with tarps;
and barely reaching me
this scent of pines and deep lakes
that remains in your hands
like a memory of eternity.

5. A LYRICAL REVERIE

When the time approached for lovers to go,
then only music, like the premonition of a train station
will bring the memory of the golden shoulders of a woman that,
on the backdrop of white covers,
were only like the flash of sunlight
on things left in the room.

We part somewhat sadly near the entrance
                         into the metro,
and our breath freezes in the chilly air,
awkward, like the myth of eternal love.
And only when our eyes meet
do we smile easily and simply,
and that smile,

like lit cigarettes in the night,
snatches our faces from the darkness,
and the sudden flare of eyes,
and the understanding of the fact
that our farewell —
is bright, like the music of wormwood
near a tent,
near a wandering sun.

6. A REVERIE IN AN INDUSTRIAL LANDSCAPE

Surely because
we had no old filigree clock
to strike out time on a town hall,
the rush hour
carried us in a crowded trolley bus.
And light appeared to us
where the line of the parkways
were like the hands of lovers,
and music in the bars —boisterous, like a yacht
that illuminated all the fires
and rushes among the reefs of the night
shining from sea foam.

7. A BARE REVERIE

The monotonousness of rain
like the white foam of apricots
at the hour of bloom,
the asphalt encrusts with an unbelievable luster,
and just the flashing of the stone walls echoes
like proof of the fact
that lovers come unnoticeably,
like an echo in the spectral glow of rain
with colored streams of water on wet clothing,
so that only with eyes, and not the quiet touch of lips,
to create the legend of Beatrice.

MINIATURE SKETCHES

A Cycle

1. FAR-FAR BEYOND THE CITY

To spread an old tent above the path
to knock together a table from wooden boxes.
Sweet country honey,
bitter country salt.

Soundless paths, in the fog —
an elder tree and elderberry.
Our fates are light strokes
on the coarse canvas of the heavens.

2. AN INDOLENT EVENING
(IN OLD KYIV)

Snow that falls on the hair, on arms,
circles around street lamps,
it sweeps up snowdrifts
near the entryways
and around the tram tracks...

Snow
that is like sparks of a bonfire in the night
near a lake with yellow flowers.

And you need to remain silent
about our unbelievable youth,
for today is a day of snow.
A day of poetry —
tomorrow.

3. WAITING
(IN OLD KYIV)

A coffee house in a basement.
If you wish

you can see the whole world
from its windows.

(Waitress, a coffee, please.
Why so sad today?
You have to paint Kyiv in pure colors,
green trees,
yellow buildings,
blue sky).

Who understands
our sorrows
and joys?
Waitresses in the coffee shop
have flowers instead of lips. Go and pick them.

(Your derision for me
means almost nothing.
The sun simply sets and rises).

This coffee house is so bitter —
like children's tears.
I would leave here,
but on all the roads
a vast boundless sky lies above our heads.

4. SAYING GOOD-BYE AT 6 AM
You smiled so sadly,
the way the fog lifts at dawn,
confusing the colors of posters.

You smiled sadly
and goblets sadly clanged
like a tram car on a bridge in the fog.

You smiled so sadly
as though we were parting forever.
You smiled so sadly.

5. THE WORLD
(AN EPIC MOOD)

Hundreds of threads tied us.
Pigeons
that coo on the city squares,
eyes of a lover,
bitter cherries from Oleh's Hill.

You speak to me
with the voice of people from our quarter —
locksmiths,
beggars,
truck drivers.

I look for you in the coffee houses
                              and libraries,
in lines of poetry
and the colors of paintings.

I thought about you
when times were hard.
And for you I started up a conversation
with anyone I happened to come across on the street.

...at dawn the earth is in fog,
like a woman naked
beneath a duvet.

6. AT NIGHT IN SOMEONE ELSE'S CITY

I return for the spring
to a land of enchanted castles,
where black lakes
on black waves sway
the glow of a silver moon.

Oh, the eternal sound of trains
and the eternal questions of those who returned

like the cry of wheels
beneath the sky.

7. EVENING AT THE TRAIN STATION
The irreversibility of unsaid words
and unfinished poems
are like trains
that have to move soon

...yet nothing happens,
besides a terrible emptiness
and the most beautiful faces
on the platform
that floats away.

8. DRINKING WINE
A transparent goblet,
crystal, with threads of the sun,
a golden shadow on the table
like the last mention
of sailors
who failed to return from the land of orchids.

Your lips smell of the sea.

9. TARGET PRACTICE
During the day
beneath a burning sun
in a burnt-out coarse cotton shirt
slowly raise your machine gun

and with pleasure recognize with your cheek
the lacquered cold of the rifle butt,
so that in a moment
you hold only the knocking of his hot heart
in your hands.

10. SHE REGRETTED
With cold ferocity
thrown beneath the feet a steppe turned yellow
with a thin strand of water in the east.

And the blackened Rus warriors
who walk in long pliant columns,
like a mountain
seeking Mohammed.
O earth of ours,
thou art already beyond the helmets.

11. A LITTLE BOY WALKING
(IN OLD KYIV)
He walks along the cobblestone alley
shuffling the slingshot ammo in his pocket,
the implacable enemy of candies and ice cream,
he walks and whistles —
with his torn sneakers knocking
the food out of a tin can.
Not knowing that for tomorrow
he will learn to look at this world
and love it.

He walks to something far away,
like a legend.

12. SILENCE IN RED
(IN OLD KYIV)
There will remain a thin black line
where the street ends
and the sunset floats out red and warm.

Coarse uneven cobblestones
clumsily will sway the freight trucks,
in the cabs swaying
empty iron barrels.

There will remain a street,
decorated with blue bunches of grapes,
and heavy freight trucks
that will crawl like bloody turtles.

13. NOSTALGIA
The spreading fan of rain
and the Old Testament silence of roofs

to create in your imagination
the image of a black cat on a pole
together with a sly smile
on the audacious face of the cat
and a pirate's brig

...and to listen to the legendary falling
                              of raindrops.

14. MUSIC IS A COMPLICATED THING
A purple lizard will come
and crawl onto the windowsill

two amber dots of eyes
and purple smoke
with the outlines of a lizard.

15. A PAINTING IN AND OF ITSELF
In the fall
when the glass darkens
and the trees are made of light glass
and the river — of black glass,
we open the doors of entryways
and on shuffling steps
we see glass shadows of people,
hanging across borders
and then in the smoke
the sun rises.

Already
(fiercely golden)
grass will grow,
and fusing the impossible,
from us light will be born
and we will set off on a pilgrimage
to country birches,
carefully
so as not to disturb
the glass contours of the City.

***

This is the road from occupation,
a man walks along it.
Tanks burn by the road,
and everything all around is silent.
This man – is hard,
he's already passed through hell,
and he's ready to pass through it again.
He can satisfy himself
by life itself,
he knows the value of life.
This man – is my nation.
Tanks burn long the entire horizon,
and my nation is creating itself –
and I know no such power
that can stop it.

...A man walks along the road.
With him go a handful of ashes
that lead a child by the hand.

       Let us give praise.

OTHER POEMS

MY BLONDE

1.
At a time in fall
when leaves and bits of newspapers
rustle all night in empty city squares,
we become crueler,
and our feelings –
deeper,
and there's no need to blame anyone
for the fact that everything passes
and day after day
drives us even further apart:
running is the law of the street.
Like beeswax,
we melt away in the fingers
of its motley crowd.

2.
In this park,
on its level darkened alleys,
we sensed that somewhere behind us
fall was pounding bridges with heavy rain.
A cop's flashlight
for an instant snatched out of the darkness
the strange pattern of maple branches
and a summer stage
with leaves piled knee-high,
and once again fall
muffled quieting footsteps
of the last people
who walked past us that night –
two patrolmen with a German Shepherd
along with a low-hanging rain
that began

near the Syrets TV tower
and that eventually completely hid its lights.

3.
I love you,
that's why everything got mixed up –
and the wind sways reddish trains
from end to end
throughout the country.
Yet,
of what surrounds me,
I love the scent of your perfume
and the street we're walking along,
I love to make you happy
and to come to understand
the sudden tenderness of your body,
I love our simple and precise words
that denote objects
we touch,
music for dancing and memories
and the smiles of our friends
who say that we lucked out.
But sometimes
I meet you
by accident
in a crowd
of umbrellas and damp raincoats,
I stop,
I listen to your reproaches
then invite you to spend the evening with me,
and after a time,
after we are left alone,
we grow silent,
light falls
just in semicircles
on our faces.

4.
The moment comes
when I leave work
and you're there waiting for me
on a bench near the theater.
It's cozy next to you,
like somewhere in the mountain forests,
when a campfire is smoldering
and a river is quietly gurgling.
I lower my face
into the collar of my sweater,
and the day is
sustained with coffee and cigarettes,
squabbles and fatigue
are gradually forgotten,
and instead
the street gets filled with autumn colors
of the evening,
the light gold of your hair
and the whisper of your lips
that are also tired a bit,
but so joyful for our meeting.

AN EVENING IN THE FOOTHILLS

1

The hair spread out on your shoulder slowly fell,
my hands got entangled in the blonde foam.
The station, fanciful shadows and rustling leaves,
wind sways its voice like a cypress sprig.

I see the flat roofs of houses and the mountains of Chor-Bedu
and in the dark silhouette of the road I see you somewhere,
and beyond the minarets I see white snowdrifts, train tracks,
strewn with leaves in the stone city.

Night is like the reflection of a fire that blazes in your eyes,
the thumping of wheels mixed in with the lights of coffee houses.
I'll open the door. Enter. From behind the dust
the distantly glimmering sun floats out, like a cart in the valley.

But the road is the road. Everything is thrown to the wind –
the scent of your hair, fall, a snowdrift, the wind.
Grease-spotted tables in teahouses, and a cautious wind
sways our two figures, the horizon, the towers, the wind.

2

Here, where the scent of smoke
merges with that of the wet floor and tables,
I lift the teacup to my lips, and the hot water gives comfort.
Then come memories.

The door of the teahouse is open,
people come in, like the long melody of mountains
where out of all possible lonelinesses
the loneliness of the road is chosen,

where on the roadsides donkeys saddled with burlap
pull wooden carts with wooden wheels

as if a train of Macedonian phalanxes,
lost in the twilight of the Pamir Mountains
were riding through the night.

The reddish shade of surrounding boundlessness
Lay in my eyes.
I'm beginning to love these mountains and see
the way rain paints your image on a glass pane,

as if the town's red roofs were appearing
through a fog.
We walk out slowly.
Voices, like a continuation of the rain,
roll along between the walls of the gorge.

TRANSLATIONS BY
VIRLANA TKACZ AND WANDA PHIPPS

BLOND

1.
In autumn,
as leaves and newspapers
rustle in the empty square all through the night,
we're cruel to each other
and our words
cut deep.

No one's to blame.
Time passes
and each day
throws us further apart:
that's the way of the street.

So one day
we'll just melt back into the crowd again
like wax.

2.
In the park,
sheltered by trees,
we sense autumn
pouring down heavy rain somewhere behind us.

For a moment
a policeman's flashlight reveals
the curious design of the maple trees
and the summer stage,
now covered knee-deep in leaves.

Then again autumn
stifles the steps
of the officer and his dog

and the rain clouds
hide the lights of the radio tower.

3.
I love you
because everything's mixed up —
the wind rattles red trains
all over the country
from one end to the other.
And most of all,
I love the smell of your perfume
and the pavement we're walking on.

I love to make you happy,
to feel that sudden tenderness of your body.

I love our simple and precise words
that define the objects
which we touch,
the music we dance to, our memories,
and the smiles of friends
who say that we lucked out.

But there are times when
I meet you
only by accident
in a crowd,
among umbrellas and coats wet with rain.
I stop,
and listen to your reproaches,
and ask you to spend the evening with me,
but then,
as the street empties out
we fall silent
and shadows carve
half circles
on our faces.

4.
Evening arrives,
I leave work
and find you sitting on a bench,
waiting for me.

Silence surrounds you.
You could be in the mountains,
sitting by a smoky fire,
listening to a stream.

I lower my face
into my sweater
and day's cigarettes and coffee,
arguments and exhaustion,
slowly fade
as the street fills
with the colors of autumn,
with the golden light of your hair,
and the whispers on your lips.
We're tired,
but glad that we've met.

5.
... We talk with friends:
the voices of the women
disappear
in the crisp air
of Indian summer.

The colors evoke illusion:
the sun seen through spider webs,
the car horn heard through plate glass,
the memories of a night so silent
you could hear the ticking of a clock,
when you opened yourself to love,
and then your barely audible voice
rocked the whole world and us
in the web of an autumn morning.

A BRIDGE CROSSES THE POND

A bridge crosses the pond
in the garden of our youth
once there was no bridge
once there was no town
there was only daylight
and our garden.

FLYING SOUTH THROUGH THE NIGHT

Flying south through the night
On the highway of dreams
In the blue dust of the road
Your sweetheart at your side.
To recognize her after a hundred years
On the knife's edge
In the valley of long rains
In the music of thunderstorms;
Or late at night in a cafe
In the fragile sorrow
Of a blue glance
Softened by shadows.
After one hundred years
To recognize her in the music
In the light silhouette of a wing
In the glow of a glance.
And then as you pass her
Whisper "You're mine."
Flying south through the night...

BEATLES

(A cycle)

      1.
I want to tell you about
how we loved each other,
queen of my life when I was sixteen.

We would see each other
in our garden,
and there was school,
and there were factory shifts,
and there were underaged beauty queens
ready to take on the whole world in love,
because
our block
stood in the sun
and hot blood pulsed
in its veins.

And we made love to each other
in the garden down the block,
lying in the tall grass near the stadium,
we would listen to
our royal block fall asleep
and watch the lights
dim.
And then we'd imagine
we were not locals,
and we'd fall in love,
and we'd want to change the world,
and then our town seemed grand,
and then our love seemed grand.

      2.
When I hear this music from Liverpool
as my palm rests on your breast,

I watch desire spark
in your eyes,
and I know
that this music speaks of
a city coming to life in the morning,
as we set off for work,
as dew drips off the chestnut leaves,
when we part
I embrace you
you talk of love,
even though I'm certain
we'll never see each other again.
My town gave you to me,
but in the morning you disappear in its traffic,
and in farewell
your tangled hair flies in the wind
and your clothes
wrap round your body,
which no longer belongs to me,
but to the burning thirst of this music from Liverpool.

    3.
When I think of writing about you
words disappear.

I remember our childhood,
where between the flares of the sun —
people were busy with their own affairs
trees blossomed
and truck wheels
collected
the red dirt of the suburbs
and all the legends of the road
which was straight, bare
and disappeared into the horizon.
If we ever
set our lives to music,

it will be the music of dust, brick and petroleum,
where we were the only poetry in town.

    4.
Believe me
the Beatles —
were our youth
an open window
in the empty room of mass art
and sterilized
classical music
do you hear —
the block lives
the people, the cats and the trees live
the giant sun lives over the block
the songs live and that is why
you undress
jeans and sweater fly into the corner
and without clothes
you look like such a woman
and I love
your flowing, shy movements
and the restrained joy of premonition
that clouds your eyes.
Believe me
the Beatles
were our youth,
but we'll have to write
about our love
ourselves.

    5.
... I see the guys on our block
and I think: we'll give those Liverpool boys
a run for their money
our guitars play our own music
and our lips pronounce our own words
and maybe, they're not great yet

but they're songs about us —
about how we love
and how we learn to fight,
to break the blows,
and how we slowly grow used to the words
Struggle and Nation
and how the hearts of our lovers sound,
as they beat over the music from Liverpool
I think
our own music lives on our block
and now we are just groping for it.

SPONTANEOUS MOTION

Downpour in the projects.

In the abandoned park — you stand alone
holding a pine branch.

We go down the stairs to the pond:
to the dock —
under the willows,
we can't see the moon,
just brilliant glitter
and the blue of the pines,
as they sway on the waves.

... Your lips search me out,
wet from the evening rain...

... Cigarettes
glow on the dock...

... In a downpour in the projects
we find love...

We enter each other
wading into water.
Our fingers carelessly entwined,
and with your free hand
you lift your skirt
bunching it up into a ball.
Sinking in the branches, pine needles and leaves,
that float on the surface,
we enter deeper,
raking aside the debris
waves lap over us.

The Frontier
28 Contemporary Ukrainian Poets - An Anthology

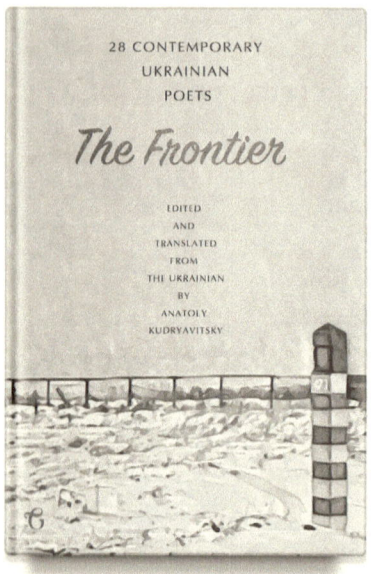

This anthology reflects a search of the Ukrainian nation for its identity, the roots of which lie deep inside Ukrainian-language poetry. Some of the included poets are well-known locally and internationally; among them are Serhiy Zhadan, Halyna Kruk, Ostap Slyvynsky, Marianna Kijanowska, Oleh Kotsarev, Anna Bagriana and, of course, the living legend of Ukrainian poetry, Vasyl Holoborodko. The next Ukrainian poetic generation also features prominently in the collection. Such poets as Les Beley, Olena Herasymyuk, Myroslav Laiuk, Hanna Malihon, Taras Malkovych, Julia Musakovska, Julia Stahivska and Lyuba Yakimchuk are the ones Ukrainians like to read today, and each of them already has an excellent reputation abroad due to festival appearances and translations to European languages. The work collected here documents poetry in Ukraine responding to challenges of the time by forging a radical new poetic, reconsidering writing techniques and language itself.

Edited and translated from the Ukrainian by Anatoly Kudryavitsky.

A Bilingual Edition.

Buy it > www.glagoslav.com

Acropolis – The Wawel Plays
by Stanisław Wyspiański

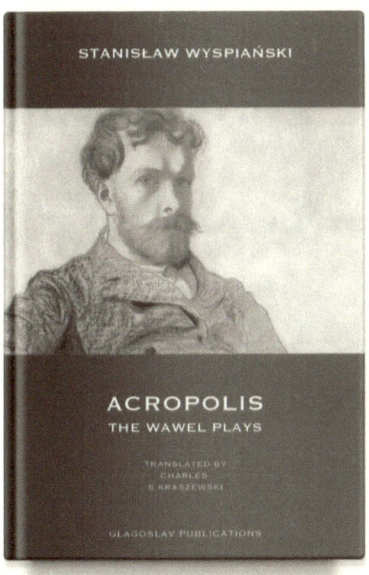

Stanisław Wyspiański (1869-1907) achieved worldwide fame, both as a painter, and Poland's greatest dramatist of the first half of the twentieth century. *Acropolis: the Wawel Plays*, brings together four of Wyspiański's most important dramatic works in a new English translation by Charles S. Kraszewski. All of the plays centre on Wawel Hill: the legendary seat of royal and ecclesiastical power in the poet's native city, the ancient capital of Poland. In these plays, Wyspiański explores the foundational myths of his nation: that of the self-sacrificial Wanda, and the struggle between King Bolesław the Bold and Bishop Stanisław Szczepanowski. In the eponymous play which brings the cycle to an end, Wyspiański carefully considers the value of myth to a nation without political autonomy, soaring in thought into an apocalyptic vision of the future. Richly illustrated with the poet's artwork, *Acropolis: the Wawel Plays* also contains Wyspiański's architectural proposal for the renovation of Wawel Hill, and a detailed critical introduction by the translator. In its plaited presentation of *Bolesław the Bold* and *Skałka*, the translation offers, for the first time, the two plays in the unified, composite format that the poet intended, but was prevented from carrying out by his untimely death.

Buy it > www.glagoslav.com

Pavlo Tychyna:
The Complete Early Poetry Collections

Pavlo Tychyna (1891-1967) is arguably the greatest Ukrainian poet of the twentieth century and has been described as a "tillerman's Orpheus" by Ukrainian poet and literary critic Vasyl Barka. With his innovative poetics, deep spirituality and creative word play, Tychyna deserves a place among the pantheon of his European contemporaries such as T.S. Eliot, Ezra Pound, Rainer Maria Rilke, Federico Garcia Lorca, and Osip Mandelstam. His early collections *Clarinets of the Sun* (1918), *The Plow* (1920), *Instead of Sonnets and Octaves* (1920), The Wind from Ukraine (1924), and his poetic cycle In the Orchestra of the Cosmos (1921) mark the pinnacle of his creativity and poetically document the emotional and spiritual toll of the Revolution of 1917 as well as the Civil War and its aftermath in Ukraine.

Buy it > www.glagoslav.com

The Grand Harmony
by Bohdan Ihor Antonych

The extraordinarily inventive Ukrainian poet and literary critic Bohdan Ihor Antonych (1909-1937), the son of a Catholic priest, died prematurely at the early age of 28 of pneumonia. Originally from the mountainous Lemko region in Poland, where a variant of Ukrainian is spoken, he was home-schooled for the first eleven years of his life because of frequent illness. He began to write poetry in Ukrainian after he moved to the Western Ukrainian city of Lviv to continue his studies at the University of Lviv.

A collection of poems on religious themes written in 1932 and 1933, *The Grand Harmony* is a subtle and supple examination of Antonych's intimately personal journey to faith, with all its revelatory verities as well as self-questioning and doubt. The collection marks the beginning of Antonych's development into one of the greatest poets of his time.

Buy it > www.glagoslav.com

Tsunami

by Anatoly Kurchatkin

Anatoly Kurchatkin's novel, set in Russia and Thailand, ranges in time from the Brezhnev years of political stagnation, when Soviet values seemed set to endure for eternity, through Gorbachev's Perestroika and the following tumultuous and disorientating decades. Under the surface, ancient currents are influencing the destinies of mathematician Rad, art gallery owner Jenny, entrepreneur (and spy?) Dron, American investor Chris, redundant Soviet diplomat Yelena and Thai playboy Tony in a rapidly globalizing world of laptop computers, mobile phones, credit cards and international finance. The fourteenth-century battle in which the Prince of Muscovy, inspired by St Sergius of Radonezh, defeated the Golden Horde of the Mongol Empire foreshadows a modern struggle for the soul of Russia.

Tsunami was shortlisted for the Russian Booker Prize and the Russo-Italian Moscow-Penne Prize.

Buy it > www.glagoslav.com

Dear Reader,

Thank you for purchasing this book.

We at Glagoslav Publications are glad to welcome you, and hope that you find our books to be a source of knowledge and inspiration.

We want to show the beauty and depth of the Slavic region to everyone looking to expand their horizon and learn something new about different cultures, different people, and we believe that with this book we have managed to do just that.

Now that you've got to know us, we want to get to know you. We value communication with our readers and want to hear from you! We offer several options:

– Join our Book Club on Goodreads, Library Thing and Shelfari, and receive special offers and information about our giveaways;

– Share your opinion about our books on Amazon, Barnes & Noble, Waterstones and other bookstores;

– Join us on Facebook and Twitter for updates on our publications and news about our authors;

– Visit our site www.glagoslav.com to check out our Catalogue and subscribe to our Newsletter.

Glagoslav Publications is getting ready to release a new collection and planning some interesting surprises — stay with us to find out!

Glagoslav Publications
Email: contact@glagoslav.com

Glagoslav Publications Catalogue

- *The Time of Women* by Elena Chizhova
- *Andrei Tarkovsky: The Collector of Dreams* by Layla Alexander-Garrett
- *Andrei Tarkovsky - A Life on the Cross* by Lyudmila Boyadzhieva
- *Sin* by Zakhar Prilepin
- *Hardly Ever Otherwise* by Maria Matios
- *Khatyn* by Ales Adamovich
- *The Lost Button* by Irene Rozdobudko
- *Christened with Crosses* by Eduard Kochergin
- *The Vital Needs of the Dead* by Igor Sakhnovsky
- *The Sarabande of Sara's Band* by Larysa Denysenko
- *A Poet and Bin Laden* by Hamid Ismailov
- *Watching The Russians (Dutch Edition)* by Maria Konyukova
- *Kobzar* by Taras Shevchenko
- *The Stone Bridge* by Alexander Terekhov
- *Moryak* by Lee Mandel
- *King Stakh's Wild Hunt* by Uladzimir Karatkevich
- *The Hawks of Peace* by Dmitry Rogozin
- *Harlequin's Costume* by Leonid Yuzefovich
- *Depeche Mode* by Serhii Zhadan
- *The Grand Slam and other stories (Dutch Edition)* by Leonid Andreev
- *METRO 2033 (Dutch Edition)* by Dmitry Glukhovsky
- *METRO 2034 (Dutch Edition)* by Dmitry Glukhovsky
- *A Russian Story* by Eugenia Kononenko
- *Herstories, An Anthology of New Ukrainian Women Prose Writers*
- *The Battle of the Sexes Russian Style* by Nadezhda Ptushkina
- *A Book Without Photographs* by Sergey Shargunov
- *Down Among The Fishes* by Natalka Babina
- *disUNITY* by Anatoly Kudryavitsky
- *Sankya* by Zakhar Prilepin
- *Wolf Messing* by Tatiana Lungin
- *Good Stalin* by Victor Erofeyev

- *Solar Plexus* by Rustam Ibragimbekov
- *Don't Call me a Victim!* by Dina Yafasova
- *Poetin (Dutch Edition)* by Chris Hutchins and Alexander Korobko
- *A History of Belarus* by Lubov Bazan
- *Children's Fashion of the Russian Empire* by Alexander Vasiliev
- *Empire of Corruption - The Russian National Pastime* by Vladimir Soloviev
- *Heroes of the 90s - People and Money. The Modern History of Russian Capitalism*
- *Fifty Highlights from the Russian Literature (Dutch Edition)* by Maarten Tengbergen
- *Bajesvolk (Dutch Edition)* by Mikhail Khodorkovsky
- *Tsarina Alexandra's Diary (Dutch Edition)*
- *Myths about Russia* by Vladimir Medinskiy
- *Boris Yeltsin - The Decade that Shook the World* by Boris Minaev
- *A Man Of Change - A study of the political life of Boris Yeltsin*
- *Sberbank - The Rebirth of Russia's Financial Giant* by Evgeny Karasyuk
- *To Get Ukraine* by Oleksandr Shyshko
- *Asystole* by Oleg Pavlov
- *Gnedich* by Maria Rybakova
- *Marina Tsvetaeva - The Essential Poetry*
- *Multiple Personalities* by Tatyana Shcherbina
- *The Investigator* by Margarita Khemlin
- *The Exile* by Zinaida Tulub
- *Leo Tolstoy – Flight from paradise* by Pavel Basinsky
- *Moscow in the 1930* by Natalia Gromova
- *Laurus (Dutch edition)* by Evgenij Vodolazkin
- *Prisoner* by Anna Nemzer
- *The Crime of Chernobyl - The Nuclear Goulag* by Wladimir Tchertkoff
- *Alpine Ballad* by Vasil Bykau
- *The Complete Correspondence of Hryhory Skovoroda*

- *The Tale of Aypi* by Ak Welsapar
- *Selected Poems* by Lydia Grigorieva
- *The Fantastic Worlds of Yuri Vynnychuk*
- *The Garden of Divine Songs and Collected Poetry of Hryhory Skovoroda*
- *Adventures in the Slavic Kitchen: A Book of Essays with Recipes*
- *Seven Signs of the Lion* by Michael M. Naydan
- *Forefathers' Eve* by Adam Mickiewicz
- *One-Two* by Igor Eliseev
- *Girls, be Good* by Bojan Babić
- *Time of the Octopus* by Anatoly Kucherena
- *Soghomon Tehlirian Memories - The Assassination of Talaat*
- *The Grand Harmony* by Bohdan Ihor Antonych
- *The Selected Lyric Poetry Of Maksym Rylsky*
- *The Shining Light* by Galymkair Mutanov
- *The Frontier: 28 Contemporary Ukrainian Poets - An Anthology*
- *Acropolis - The Wawel Plays* by Stanisław Wyspiański
- *Zinnober's Poppets* by Elena Chizhova
- *The Hemingway Game* by Evgeni Grishkovets

More coming soon...

www.ingramcontent.com/pod-product-compliance
Lightning Source LLC
Chambersburg PA
CBHW031119080526
44587CB00011B/1035